Augmented Reality

Augmented Reality

An Emerging Technologies Guide to AR

First Edition

Gregory Kipper

Joseph Rampolla

AMSTERDAM • BOSTON • HEIDELBERG • LONDON
NEW YORK • OXFORD • PARIS • SAN DIEGO
SAN FRANCISCO • SINGAPORE • SYDNEY • TOKYO

ELSEVIER

Syngress is an Imprint of Elsevier

SYNGRESS.

Acquiring Editor: Chris Katsaropoulos
Development Editor: Ben Rearick
Project Manager: Andre Cuello
Designer: Kristen Davis

Syngress is an imprint of Elsevier
225 Wyman Street, Waltham, MA 02451, USA

Library of Congress Cataloging-in-Publication Data
Application submitted

British Library Cataloguing-in-Publication Data
A catalogue record for this book is available from the British Library.

ISBN: 978-1-59749-733-6

Printed and bound by CPI Group (UK) Ltd, Croydon, CR0 4YY

Transferred to digital print 2012

For information on all Syngress publications visit our werbsite at www.syngress.com

"To my admirably patient wife Amber for enduring this whole process yet again, and to my wonderful children – Azure, McCoy, and Grant"
– Greg Kipper

"To my loving wife Pamela, and my children – Stephen, Meghan, and Sean"
– Joe Rampolla

Contents

Acknowledgments

Gregory Kipper

My thanks to Joe Rampolla, for giving a great speech and igniting the spark that started this whole adventure. To the team at Syngress for their help and patience. To Jason, Melissa, Tracey, and Marie at Total Immersion for your support during the writing process. To Jim Jaeger, Bob Browning, and Brian Carron for their confidence and support. To John Stockman, Denny Poindexter, Jason Roybal, and Lynda Mann for reviewing the book with such care on such short notice.

My extra thanks to Lt Gen William Lord, Maj Gen David Commons, and RADM Robert Day for all the thought inspiring conversations over the past two years and to Daniel Suarez for writing such a great introduction.

Joe Rampolla

To Gregory Kipper for approaching me to team up to write this book and his tireless work to make it happen, Elsevier and Syngress Publishing, Carole Mazzucco, Thomas P. Mazzucco, Dr. Robert J. Hawley, James Patrick Rampolla, Angie Liguori, Dave Kramer, Andy Yeager, Joseph Madden, Daniel Suarez for his tremendous support, Ori Inbar, Tish Shute, Helen Papagiannis, Brian Wassom, Dr. Steven Feiner, Chris Grayson, Dr. Edward Roche, Kevin Manson, David Griesbach, Bill Walsh, Dallas Crimes Against Children Conference gurus, Peter Banks, National Center for Missing and Exploited Children, Fox Valley Technical College, Cammy Newell, US Department of Justice, United States Attorney's Office, Park Ridge Police Department, Borough of Park Ridge, Bergen County Prosecutor's Office, Andre DiMino, Michael Taylor, John Paige, Charlie McKenna, Ed Moore, New Jersey Office of Homeland Security and Preparedness, Augmented Reality Group of New York (ARNY), Fox Valley Technical College (FVTC), National District Attorney's Association (NDAA), Justin Fitzsimmons, National Crimes Against Children Task Force, Maria Ugarte, Bilateral Safety Corridor Coalition (BSCC), John Jay College of Criminal Justice, Stan White, Dan Fabrizio, Erik Villanueva, Harmonie Ponder, Bobby Simpson, Eric Huber, Mark Kirk, Mike Zimmerman, Andre Ludwig, Jay Logan, Chris Sedlacik, Richard Ruiz, Augmented Reality Dirt fans, and Cyber warriors across the globe.

About the Authors

Gregory Kipper: Gregory Kipper is a futurist, author, and strategic forecaster in emerging technologies. Mr. Kipper has been the keynote speaker at select industry events, a digital forensics instructor, and a trusted advisor in both the government and commercial sectors. He has written multiple books in the fields of digital forensics and emerging technologies, including *Investigator's Guide to Steganography, Wireless Crime and Forensic Investigation,* and *Virtualization and Forensics*.

Joseph Rampolla: Joseph Rampolla, a law enforcement officer for 17 years, is a nationally recognized speaker on the topics of cyber crime, augmented reality, virtual worlds, counterterrorism, cyberbullying, and undercover Internet Relay Chat (IRC) investigations. Rampolla serves as a consultant for various organizations across the United States and presents for the National District Attorney's Association (NDAA) and Fox Valley Technical College.

Foreword

Augmented reality (AR) is a technology whose time has come. Conceived in rudimentary form as early as the 1960's, AR is only now becoming truly practical. Recent advances in mobile processing, coupled with an explosion in digital storage capacity, ubiquity of wireless broadband connections, mass adoption of smart phones, and the limitless data store that the Internet has gathered all the prerequisites for this potentially game-changing technology. Consumer AR applications are already present on hundreds of millions of smart phones (utilizing built-in cameras, accelerometers, microphones, and GPS), and with the development of new AR-specific chipsets from major chip companies like Nvidia and QualComm, the AR price-point, and the bar for entry to potential AR app-developers will be lowered further. In short: a critical mass is forming to support augmented reality products and services as a major tech/media industry.

But what is AR—and more importantly, what will be the consequences to human society when augmented reality applications go mainstream? What will be the risks and rewards? At present AR is being treated as a novelty—used to attract young eyeballs for softdrink, video game, and movie ads. However, as a three-dimensional cousin of the Internet, AR is likely to travel a similar path from novelty, to over-hyped panacea and threat, and finally to massive utility and foundational infrastructure. Along the way, individuals and companies who blaze a trail will rise and fall, but the demonstrated usefulness of AR to a broad variety of human activities augurs well for the industry's future.

It's no coincidence that one of the biggest potential uses for AR is also where the Internet shines: in democratizing access to information. This goes beyond access to trivia to include serious training and education. Entire online degree programs already pepper the Internet (in fact, free online courses are now being offered by both Harvard and M.I.T.). However, AR can take training and education even further by displaying interactive information in geospatial context—greatly enhancing its usefulness. For example, rather than reading about how to operate complex equipment, one might be able to project the apparition of a world class expert onto the scene to demonstrate first hand. Likewise, in emergency situations one might be able to call up an in-place demonstration of proper CPR technique, projected over one's hands. This takes advantage of humanity's powerful ability to absorb visual information—a trait our ancestors evolved to seek out danger in their surroundings.

From entertainment to training and education, law enforcement, military, political, legal—many industries and activities stand to gain from the advent of widespread AR technology. And yet, AR is no different from any other human endeavor; there will be hazards with this new technology as well. Unintended second and third order effects of mass adoption of AR will no doubt present complex legal and social issues never before imagined—as occurred with the advent of the Internet.

For example, facial recognition, license plate readers, bluetooth ID's, and a host of other de-anonymizing technologies coupled with an AR headset could make it possible for individuals navigating a public street to instantly retrieve detailed information on people passing by. From criminals looking for likely marks to advertisers, to law enforcement, to employers evaluating job applicants. What are the legal and social implications of the vast stores of data held about us—in the past most likely available on the Internet—but now literally hovering above our heads in a dimension visible only to certain members of society but not others? What will be the disclosure rules for passive monitoring of passers-by? Is there a reasonable expectation of privacy against data-mining in public even though a shallower privacy is not expected? What are the liability issues for the manufacturers and developers of AR games whose products might obscure actual reality enough for players to get hit by a bus? Likewise, criminals are the quintessential early adopters, always seeking advantage by being the first to try tools that might give them an unfair advantage. It is a good bet that AR will be utilized in confidence schemes to act out the latest version of the 'Nigerian Prince' scam, this time on a sidewalk with a 'long-lost friend' you have just bumped into who seems to remember ever single thing about you—even though you cannot place them. Likewise with expert knowledge; does that person you are speaking to really know Coleridge's 'Rime of the Ancient Mariner' by heart, or are they simply reading from an AR teleprompter to impress you? What if that is your lawyer speaking in your defense while in court? Would AR make it less likely to matter if a person actually *knows* something as long as they can reference the information quickly?

The social trust that binds society is about to be tested by AR even as our own capabilities are expanded by its usefulness. For both adherents to AR technology and those who need to understand its impacts, now is the time to delve into these possibilities. Reading this book will give you a head start.

Daniel Suarez

What Is Augmented Reality?

THE DEFINITION OF AUGMENTED REALITY

Augmented Reality (AR) is a variation of a Virtual Environment (VE), or Virtual Reality (VR) as it is more commonly called. Virtual Reality technologies completely immerse a user inside a synthetic environment and while immersed, the user cannot see the real world around him. In contrast, Augmented Reality is taking digital or computer generated information, whether it be images, audio, video, and touch or haptic sensations and overlaying them over in a real-time environment. Augmented Reality technically can be used to enhance all five senses, but its most common present-day use is visual. Unlike Virtual Reality, Augmented Reality allows the user to see the real world, with virtual objects superimposed upon or composited with the real world. Therefore, AR supplements reality, rather than completely replacing it as depicted in Figure 1.1 Augmented Reality can be thought of as the blend, or the "middle ground," between the completely synthetic and the completely real.

One of the easiest examples is a heads-up display, or HUD, used by fighter pilots. It is likely we have all seen examples of a HUD in movies or television documentaries. A HUD gives the pilot a digital overlay that shows an artificial horizon, the digital altitude, digital speed, and other information while looking out the cockpit window as shown in Figure 1.2 Another example that has appeared in the past few years is the artificial "first down" line Figure 1.3 that helps football viewers watching the game on TV know how far the offensive team needs to go to get a first down.

FIGURE 1.1 A 3D Graphic or Model is Superimposed on the Real-World Object Through the Use of a Smartphone

FIGURE 1.2 Fighter Jet Heads-up Display

These examples are somewhat straightforward compared to some of what we will explore in the rest of this book.

Augmented Reality can also be used to remove real-world information, not just add to it. A basic example is this the Vulcan Tourism Transporter App that creates the transporter "beaming" effect from the Star Trek series. A person sitting or object

FIGURE 1.3 An Augmented "First Down" Line

FIGURE 1.4 The AR Transporter Room Application Removes a Physical Object from View

put in front of the transporter pad can be dematerialized or rematerialized using Augmented Reality as depicted in Figure 1.4.

Building on the basic definition and descriptions of AR's capabilities let us expand a bit further and outline the three characteristics that need to be present for true Augmented Reality:

1. AR combines real and virtual information.
2. AR is interactive in real time.
3. AR operates and is used in a 3D environment.

Augmented Reality really allows for information to be presented visually that the user would not otherwise be able to detect. Just as there are millions of bits of information being transmitted all around us right now on some wireless frequency or another, we as people would be totally unaware of it without the mobile phones, tablets, and laptops that allow us to effectively channel the information. *Augmented Reality, much like other graphical interfaces, gives us the ability to bring usable information into the visual spectrum in real time wherever we are.* Augmented Reality is not just one technology. It is the combination of several technologies that work together to bring digital information into visual perception. AR is a highly compelling, virtually endless, collection of technology-assisted experiences that helps create the real-time Web.

As Gene Becker of Lightning Laboratories puts it, Augmented Reality is:

- a technology.
- a field of research.
- a vision of future computing.
- an emerging commercial industry.
- a new medium for creative expression.

Interestingly enough the same list could have, and may have, been applied to the 2D graphical user interface that became popular in the 1980s.

What AR is Not

There are more than enough examples today of digitally enhanced media, however it does not necessarily mean that all of them constitute "augmented" reality. An image altered in Photoshop, or any other type of 2D overlay, is not AR. It also does not include film or television. While movies such as "Jurassic Park" and "Avatar" feature photorealistic virtual objects seamlessly blended with a real environment in 3D, they are not interactive and thus not AR. In contrast, the football game example mentioned earlier uses a live feed and computers to create a virtual line of scrimmage on the display in real time does constitute AR, whereas a motion picture that is carefully scripted, filmed, and processed does not.

Augmented Reality is sometimes confused with "visual searching", particularly in a mobile environment. Visual searching is defined as an active scan of the visual environment for a particular object or feature among other objects or features. Programs such as Google Goggles and Nokia's Point and Find allow the user to search from their cell phones by capturing an image and finding relevant information about that image. In some ways it begins the same way AR does with "recognition" of an object and it is interactive in real time but it fails to meet the rules of actually combining real and virtual information and operating in a 3D environment.

THE COMPONENTS OF AUGMENTED REALITY

Now that we've covered the basics of what Augmented Reality is, and isn't we'll start digging a little deeper into the technology and learn about all the pieces that make AR work. There are a number of necessary components to make the whole process work as well as the different types of platforms that can be used for Augmented Reality. In Chapter Two we'll explore what makes Augmented Reality work in greater detail but for now the list below is a summary of the core components needed for both fixed and mobile environments:

Hardware:

- a computer, either a PC or a mobile device
- a monitor or display screen
- a camera
- tracking and sensing systems (GPS, compass, accelerometer)
- a network infrastructure
- a marker: markers are physical objects or places where the real and Virtual Environments are fused together. This is what the computer identifies as the place where digital information is to be presented.

Software:

- an app or program running locally
- Web services
- a content server

Augmented Reality Platforms

Now that we've touched on the necessary components here are four platforms by which Augmented Reality is used today. They are:

1. *Personal Computers with Webcams:* Since most PCs contain some, if not all, the needed components for viewing Augmented Reality on this platform are an obvious choice. Because of the fixed nature of the device (compared to mobile phones and tablets), a marker is placed within view of a Webcam, which shows a live feed. Once it identifies the marker, it creates the augmentation on the screen for the user to interact with as shown in Figure 1.5 This method is often used to augment magazine advertisements, business cards, baseball cards, and almost anything else that could be made into a portable marker and placed in front of the Webcam. Gaming systems such as the XBox are also starting to be used more and more for Augmented Reality.
2. *Kiosks, Digital Signage, and Window Displays:* Kiosks are simply stations where customers can bring items to find out more about them with Augmented Reality information. One example is the Lego Store kiosk, which displays the completed Lego set inside the box. Kiosks are also used at trade shows and conventions to give attendees a richer experience as depicted in Figure 1.6 Digital signs and window display are also used and are basically large static markers that users interact with via their mobile devices.
3. *Smartphones and Tablets:* The use of smartphones to access Augmented Reality content is arguably the most common method today. Smartphones can not

FIGURE 1.5 An Augmented Reality Greeting Card is Enabled Using a Webcam and Personal Computer

FIGURE 1.6 An AR Kiosk Gives This Person a Full View of a New Car

only use their cameras and screens to identify markers they are pointed at but can also use the compass and GPS functions to augment the locations or points of interest based on relative location (Figure 1.7). Tablet computers also fall under this general platform category as many of the higher-end models on the market today have HD cameras and GPS capability.

4. *AR Glasses and Head-Mounted Displays:* While not yet common, AR-enabled glasses such as those made by Vuzix do exist and are available for purchase. In time, as the technology improves and prices come down, AR-enabled glasses

FIGURE 1.7 An AR Application on This Smartphone Displays directions and Points of Interest

FIGURE 1.8 A Representation of What a User Could See While Wearing AR Glasses

will likely become as common as iPads and smartphones giving the wearer the option for a continuous Augmented Reality feed based on individual needs and preferences (Figure 1.8).

A BRIEF HISTORY OF AUGMENTED REALITY

There have been many talented and dedicated people who did great things with Augmented Reality with far less of a technological advantage that we enjoy in present day. The next section outlines some of those people and some of the significant events in Augmented Reality development:

1962

Morton Heilig, a cinematographer, designs a motorcycle simulator called Sensorama (Figure 1.9) which stands as one of the earliest known examples of immersive, multi-sensory technology that had visuals, sound, vibration, and smell.

FIGURE 1.9 The Sensorama

1968

Ivan Sutherland creates the first Augmented Reality (and Virtual Reality) system called The Sword of Damocles (Figure 1.10). It used an optical see-through head-mounted display and was one of the earliest examples that used six degrees-of-freedom (6DOF) trackers.

1975

Videoplace, created by Myron Krueger, who is considered one of the original pioneers of Virtual Reality and interactive art created an Augmented Reality system which allowed users to interact with virtual objects for the first time (Figure 1.11).

1992

At Boeing's Computer Services' Adaptive Neural Systems Research and Development project, Tom Caudell and David Mizell are credited with coining the term "Augmented Reality." This came about from their R&D work which centered around an effort to find an easier way to help Boeing's manufacturing and engineering process which led them to design software that could overlay the positions of where certain cables in the building process were supposed to go.

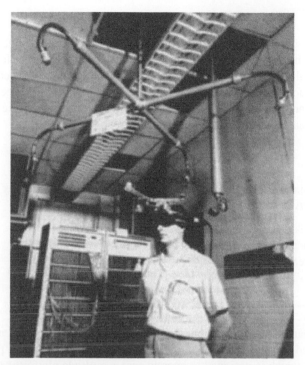

FIGURE 1.10 The Sword of Damocles Optical Head-Mounted Display

FIGURE 1.11 Videoplace

1996

Jun Rekimoto develops an AR prototype called NaviCam and advances the idea of the 2D matrix marker (Figure 1.12). Markers are physical objects or places where the real and Virtual Environment are fused together. A marker is what the computer identifies as the place where digital information is to be presented. This type becomes one of the first marker systems to allow camera tracking with six degrees-of-freedom. This type of marker is still in use today.

1997

Ronald Azuma, a research leader in Augmented Reality, provides the de facto definition for AR, as identified by these three characteristics.

1. It combines real and virtual.
2. It is interactive in real time.
3. It is registered in 3D.

1999

• The company, Total Immersion, is founded and enters the market as the first Augmented Reality solutions provider. Total Immersion creates a product called D'Fusion, which is designed to operate across multiple platforms and then

FIGURE 1.12 A Common 2D Augmented Reality Marker

spends the next decade on research and development establishing the company as the market leader in Augmented Reality.

- Hirokazu Kato releases the ARToolKit to the open source community. This suite of tools allows for video capture in the real world to be combined with virtual objects, to include 3D graphics, and be run on any operating system. Today almost all Flash-based AR that is seen through a Web browser was made using ARToolKit.

- Hollerer, Feiner, and Pavlik develop a wearable AR system that lets users to experience AR information that is integrated with relevant outdoor locations. This system is a prelude to the AR browser.

2000

- Bruce Thomas et al. create an AR version of the popular game Quake. "AR-Quake" depicted in Figure 1.13 was a first-person Augmented Reality view of the game which incorporated a six degrees-of-freedom (6DOF) tracking system, GPS, a digital compass, and vision-based marker tracking.

- Also in 2000, Simon Julier et al. create the "BARS" or the Battlefield Augmented Reality System (Figure 1.14). This system provided useful information relevant to the soldier on the ground. It consisted of a wearable computer, a wireless networking system, and a head-mounted display.

FIGURE 1.13 AR Quake as Seen by a Player

FIGURE 1.14 The Battlefield Augmented Reality System

FIGURE 1.15 A Multi-User AR System

2001

• Reitmayr and Schmalstieg create a mobile, multi-user AR system. This design showed the potential for AR hybrid systems by combining mobile Augmented Reality and collaboration capabilities between users in a shared Augmented Reality space as seen in Figure 1.15.

FIGURE 1.16 Archeoguide

- "Archeoguide" is created by Vlahakis et al., which is an AR system for tourism and education. Archeoguide (Figure 1.16) was built around the historical site of Olympia, Greece, and contained a navigation interface, 3D models of ancient temples and statues, and avatars competing in a run.
- The Real-World Wide Web (RWWW) Browser created by Kooper and MacIntyre is recognized as the first AR Browser. This mobile system acted as an AR interface to the World Wide Web.

2004

The first system for tracking 3D markers on mobile phones was presented by Mathias Möhring. The development allowed for the detection and differentiation of different 3D markers and the integration of 3D renderings into a live video stream. This work showed a first video see-through Augmented Reality system on a consumer cell phone.

2006

Nokia initiates the Mobile Augmented Reality Applications (MARA) project. The research project experimented with creating an AR guidance application using the multi-sensor functions in mobile phones. The prototype application overlaid a continuous viewfinder image stream captured by the camera and annotated the users surrounding in real time with graphics and text.

2008

Mobilizy launches the Wikitude World Browser with Augmented Reality. This application combines GPS and compass data with Wikipedia entries and overlays information on the real-time camera view of a smartphone.

2009

SPRXmobile launches Layar. Layar is another AR browser that uses GPS and compass data for registration. Layar uses an open client-server platform and content layers, which is an AR browser equivalent of traditional Web pages on a PC-based browser.

As we have seen in this brief, and by no means comprehensive, history of AR and mobile AR it has been a long road with many interesting developments and innovations along the way. In the next section we will begin in the present and take a brief look at some of the things Augmented Reality is being used for today.

AUGMENTED REALITY TODAY: 2012

As Augmented Reality continues to develop over the decades and works its way into the modern technological landscape of today, it is worth spending some time looking at all of the ways that Augmented Reality is being used at the time of this writing.

Advertising

Today more and more brands are leveraging the ubiquity of the mobile phone to begin integrating Augmented Reality within their campaigns. Companies such as Nissan, Toyota, BMW, and Mini are using magazine advertisements and AR to give the viewer a full 3D view of the car being advertised. Lego stores use an AR system to provide kids an animated version of the completed Lego set inside the box they are holding. The motion picture industry has also taken advantage of Augmented Reality to promote movies such as Transformers, Iron Man, and Star Trek.

One of the bigger examples is the "N Building" in the Tokyo shopping district, which is outlined in the Quick Response (QR) code section that allows shoppers and passers-by to use AR to get real-time information about what's inside the building, show Tweets that are being posted by people inside the building, and have different augmented decorations depending on the season.

Task Support

One of the biggest potential uses for Augmented Reality in the future is that of task support. AR has been, and will continue to be used to aid people to more easily carrying out complex tasks such as assembly and maintenance. One example of this use of AR can be found at the US Post Office. The program lets users check the size of their packages before sending them, saving time, and making for an easier time at the Post Office. Another example is a mobile Augmented Reality printer repair application (Figure 1.17) outlining the future and the potential for AR task support to the mobile environment.

Navigation

A big use and continued potential for Augmented Reality is navigation. City guides such as Yelp and NRU (pronounced "near you") which help people find places to eat, drink, and shop have Augmented Reality capabilities that give users real-time visual directions to the places their looking for.

Another application called TapNav uses AR to overlay your route on the road ahead (Figure 1.18). The visual benefits to this are immediately obvious as you can quickly see where you are supposed to be going with easy visual cues. However, there are currently a couple of drawbacks with this concept as well. Most significantly is the danger associated with looking through a mobile phone while driving.

Home and Industrial

AR is currently being used in home and industrial environments. For home use, Total Immersion's Magic Mirror uses Augmented Reality to place and scale representations of furniture or appliances letting the viewer get a sense for how it

FIGURE 1.17 An Augmented Reality Printer Maintenance Program

FIGURE 1.18 The TapNav Display

FIGURE 1.19 Augmented Reality Being Used to Show the Placement of a New Television

looks (Figure 1.19). The same application could also be used for larger projects such as comparing digital mock-ups with physical mock-ups to find any discrepancies between them.

Art

Augmented Reality artwork is another variant that exists today. An app called Konstruct allows you to generate artwork in an AR environment (Figure 1.20). In 2010 New York's Museum of Modern Art hosted an exhibit that allowed anyone with an iPhone or Android phone to view "hidden" exhibitions in Augmented Reality.

FIGURE 1.20 The AR Application "Konstruct" Lets a Museum Visitor Create an Interactive Work of Art

Sightseeing

Since sightseeing is literally just that, AR is perfect for an enhanced sightseeing experience. By unlocking hidden, and interesting, information that is all around, the tourist, sightseer, or academic will have the chance to explore the unique details of a place. There are currently a couple of AR applications specifically designed for tourism. One of them is called "Tuscany + Augmented Reality" which brings up points of interest for the traveler in Tuscany. Another example is the Virtual Sightseeing scenic viewer located at the Environmental Interpretation Center at Ponta do Sal. This non-mobile AR experience offers visitors the chance to explore the uniqueness of the Cascais coastal biodiversity and man-made landmarks (Figure 1.21).

Entertainment and Games

The entertainment and gaming industries in the United States are nothing short of massive, generating billions of dollars every year. PricewaterhouseCoopers forecast that the worldwide gaming revenues in 2012 would reach just over $68 Billion. As with any new compelling technology, producers, and entertainers have always gravitated towards something that will make for a better experience for audiences. With the continued growth of the mobile market, producers, and entertainment companies are also reexamining what entertainment means for audiences on the go. Augmented Reality has tremendous potential going forward where the technology will allow people to interact with their entertainment wherever they go and based on their location.

There are currently dozens of AR-enabled games available for mobiles and desktop computers. Simply searching for "Augmented Reality" on iTunes reveals dozens of mobile games for just about every interest, and more are being released all the time.

FIGURE 1.21 The Virtual Sightseeing Station at Ponta do Sal

FIGURE 1.22 An iPad Controlling a Parrot AR.Drone

The Parrot AR.Drone (Figure 1.22) is another example and combines a flying remote controlled toy with an iPhone or iPad app. When the app is installed, the iPhone or iPad uses the accelerometer and touch interface to become a remote control for the Parrot Drone. Adding to this, there is also a camera on the Drone which lets the user view things from the Drone's point of view and allowing the user to have virtual dogfights with other Drones.

Augmented Reality has also been used to enhance concert and theater performances. One example is the "Duran Duran Project," where the band used AR on stage to create new effects for the audience. AR is also starting to become new media for interactive movies, but we'll discuss that in Chapter 3.

Social Networking

With the ever-growing use of social networking sites and the quickly growing popularity of mobile social networking it's no real surprise that Augmented Reality is being used to create richer social networking experiences. An example of this is a mobile app prototype called "Recognizr" that allows you to use your phone in order to "see" who a person is and what Web services and social networks they are connected to Figure 1.23.

Education

Information technology is changing education in a number of ways. Beginning simply with the amount of information that is now available to everyone with access to the Internet, to online learning methods, and interactive interfaces such as the Promethean Board which lets students interact with a digital "chalkboard" in ways that the old chalkboard couldn't (Figure 1.24).

Augmented Reality appeals to the education approach that students learn the most when they take control of their own learning and interact with the real and augmented environments. With Augmented Reality students can manipulate virtual objects or representations of real objects that would otherwise be impossible to hold as well as

FIGURE 1.23 The "Recognizr" Augmented Reality Social Networking app

FIGURE 1.24 A Student Interacting With a Promethean Board

learn tasks and skills. The benefit with AR learning is that there are no *real* errors only various degrees of learning experiences. AR also has tremendous potential for advanced education and maintaining a set of skills. For example, mechanics could learn repair procedures on a new piece of equipment, a firefighter could learn how to fight specific types of virtualized fires. Beyond the blended nature of the training the other value is that there are no lasting consequences if mistakes are made. Any mistakes that might be made would only provide opportunities for more real-time feedback and authentic learning while appealing to multiple learning styles.

Translation

Optical character recognition has improved steadily over the years and an outgrowth of this has led to the development of an Augmented Reality translator. The user simply points a smartphone at the text he or she wishes to translate and the answer appears on the screen. Word Lens is one such AR translation application (Figure 1.25) that reads the text visible in the camera window, translates it, and then overlays the original text with the translation. Another program, called Intelligent Eye, operates much the same way.

THE DIFFERENCES BETWEEN AUGMENTED REALITY AND VIRTUAL REALITY

In this section we'll look closely at the technical differences and similarities between Augmented Reality, Virtual Reality, and quick response codes. While they all share some commonalities and often inter-relate, they are, in the end, distinct technologies.

FIGURE 1.25 The WorldLens Augmented Reality Translator

What is Virtual Reality?

Virtual Reality is a completely artificial digital environment that uses computer hardware and software to create the appearance of a real environment to the user. For a user to "enter" a Virtual Reality environment they must first put on special gloves, earphones, and goggles, all of which receive their input from the computer system (Figure 1.26). By doing this at least three of the five senses are controlled by the computer. In addition, the computer monitors the user's actions. The goggles, for example, track how the eyes

FIGURE 1.26 A Virtual Reality Flight Simulator System

move and respond accordingly by sending new video input. Virtual Reality enjoyed a lot of hype in the 1990s but fizzled out rather quickly by the end of that decade.

Similarities and Differences Between VR and AR

Virtual Reality is the complete immersion into a digital world either based on a real model or completely fabricated. Augmented Reality is the blending of digital information within a real-world environment. The similarities between the two are that they both use various sources of information and programming to create visual, or other sensory, simulations to create an experience. In spite of the similarities in feel to the user, there are more differences between AR and VR than there are similarities, with the biggest difference being that one takes place in the real world and the other does not.

THE DIFFERENCE BETWEEN AR AND QR CODES

A QR code (abbreviation for Quick Response code) is a two-dimensional code that is readable by either a QR barcode reader or smartphones. The code consists of black modules arranged in a square pattern on a white background. The QR code was created to allow its contents to be decoded at high speed. The information encoded may be text, URL, or general information such as on business cards, a video, SMS text message and so on. In order to use a mobile for QR code, the phone will require an app reader.

   Common in Japan, the QR code is one of the most popular types of two-dimensional barcodes and this popularity has spread to the United States in the past few years appearing more and more in magazine advertisements and product packaging Figure 1.27

FIGURE 1.27 QR Code on a Soft Drink Bottle

CHALLENGES WITH AR

In this section we'll explore some of the challenges with Augmented Reality and they are broken out into two categories: technical and social. Technical challenges examine things like the recognition problem and sensory accuracy as well as authoring limitations that stem from different hardware and software platforms and usage issues such as location and position. Social challenges explore the issues that don't tie directly to the technology supporting AR, but rather some of the potentially negative side effects of using AR.

Technical Challenges of Augmented Reality

As with any complex system, one requiring multiple components to work properly in order for the system to function, there will always be problems. AR systems are no different. While many of the challenges with the technical components of AR are continually being improved upon, as of this writing, the biggest technical challenges affecting AR are object recognition and sensor accuracy.

Object recognition or the "registration" problem is one of the most basic problems currently limiting Augmented Reality applications. Objects in the real and virtual worlds must be properly aligned with respect to each other, or the illusion that the two worlds coexist will be affected, sometimes severely. (Figure 1.28). Without

FIGURE 1.28 An Example of the Registration Problem Where the Virtual Object and the Person are Not Properly Aligned

accurate registration, Augmented Reality will not be used in a variety of applications that could be greatly enhanced by having an AR component.

Sensor accuracy applies to mobile AR and the systems that support it. Modern mobile Augmented Reality systems use one or more of the following tracking technologies: digital cameras and/or other optical sensors, accelerometers, GPS, gyroscopes, solid-state compasses, RFID, and wireless sensors. These technologies offer varying levels of accuracy and precision. Indoor positioning and line-of-sight also create challenges when dealing with location-based AR.

There are other technical challenges as well such as device interoperability, authoring limitations based on specific platforms, device constraints such as the small display size in mobile phones. People may not want to rely on their cell phones, which have small screens on which to superimpose information. As iPads and other tablets continue to populate the technology landscape, their larger screens will make for a richer user experience with the ultimate goal of having AR-enabled glasses, and eventually contact lenses, to make the physical and digital experience as seamless as possible.

For AR to really be successful it must have a low-learning curve, which by its very nature is almost built in, but there will be other challenges. It must also be useful. At present AR is still being used primarily for entertainment and advertising, as this changes and it expands into education, medicine, maintenance, and other fields that are always looking for more effective methods or solutions it's likely that AR will become a regular option in our lives. I say *option* because there will be times when AR might not be the preferred choice; just as using a smartphone today isn't always applicable for every situation, such as writing a book.

Social Challenges of Augmented Reality

The social, or non-technical, challenges of AR will take more to overcome than most of the technical challenges. The reason for this is simple, if people don't like something they usually won't use it. So let's begin this section by taking a more skeptical point of view of AR and ask the question, "Will Augmented Reality every really take off?"

Using other tech savvy nations as a baseline, such as Japan, it is very likely AR will grow quite popular, especially considering new technology adoption is part of their culture. Other countries such as the United States, Europe, and the UK may have a slower adoption but the eventual integration of Augmented Reality (to some degree) is probably inevitable particularly as younger generations grow up with this technology. In the meantime, there are some real challenges AR currently faces and will continue to face in the future, especially as it matures.

The first real challenge for AR is having a wide range of excellent user experiences available to people. Currently content is somewhat obscure or appeals to a narrow range of users, however this is quickly changing. For now Augmented Reality remains largely unknown to the general public and in order for this to change a great variety of user experiences will have to be created that are functional, affordable, and have a low-learning curve.

Another challenge for AR is the issue of privacy. Since one of the core components of an AR system is a camera, its clear the camera will be "seeing" everything the user decides to point the lens at. Using facial recognition technology, such as that found in the AR app "Viewdle," combined with geo-location and augmented data will potentially lead to a seamless integration of our online and offline activities. This means a person walking around in the physical world will no longer just be a person, they will become part of the "Internet of Things" (described in Chapter 6), with a digital profile and whatever other information the person chooses to make available online. This type of scenario was described in the fiction thriller "Freedom ^{TM}" by Daniel Suarez in which a character in the story, using AR-enabled glasses, was able to look at people walking down the street, identify them, and then display private information about them. In the story it was each person's net worth represented as a positive or negative dollar figure floating over their head. While this example is extreme, and may have just given you pause as you read it, it is also well within the realm of possibility today.

A third challenge is the risk of real physical safety. Mobile phones are currently a serious distraction while driving a car accounting for thousands of accidents, injuries, and deaths each year on the road. A 2005 study conducted by the University of Utah discovered that cell phone distraction causes 2600 deaths and 330,000 injuries in the United States every year. An augmented windshield that presents you with driving directions has clear benefits if developed properly. However if such a windshield could deliver driving directions, it is safe to speculate that it will be capable of feeding the driver all sorts of additional information, information the driver may not need. At that point, for all intents and purposes, the windshield could be viewed the same way a computer monitor is today, with numerous windows displaying different types of information. The challenge then becomes that one of those windows is the actual open road. Considering the effect mobile phone usage has on driving it's not difficult to imagine a driver becoming overwhelmed with information in this instance if they happen to be in an unfamiliar neighborhood using an Augmented Reality interface or windshield to look for a restaurant they're trying to find while being sent advertisements and coupons based on their location all the while trying to read a text message that just appeared (Figure 1.29).

Another challenge, especially as it becomes more and more prevalent, is that of unauthorized augmented advertising. As we have already touched on, AR has caught the attention of marketers and advertisers. The possibilities of capitalizing on spaces in the physical world by augmenting digital advertisements onto them in real time will be too big, and too lucrative, for advertisers to ignore. An extreme example of this can be seen in the movie "Minority Report" where John Anderton (played by Tom Cruise) is bombarded on a second-by-second basis with personalized advertisements for each store he passes while walking through a shopping mall. Hopefully it will never come to this and it is very possible as AR continues to evolve there will be controls in place that will prevent advertisers from augmenting their marketing messages on building surfaces, walls, and other physical objects without adequate permission. Offshoots of this challenge include unwelcome, individual ad targeting based on a person's real-world behavior by combining geolocation data and self-disclosed social media information Figure 1.30.

FIGURE 1.29 A Conceptual Rendition of an Overcrowded Augmented Reality Windshield

FIGURE 1.30 A Conceptual Rendition of Extreme AR Advertising

THE OPPORTUNITIES FOR AUGMENTED REALITY

Though it has been under development for over four decades, 2009 is widely considered the year that Augmented Reality technology became mainstream. The current hype surrounding this technology is similar to previous tech hype in the past; Virtual Reality during the 1990s and 3D online communities, such as Second Life, during the 2000s. For those technologies neither of them really lived up to the hype and many consumers stopped using them after the novelty wore off.

Augmented Reality is, and may continue to, go through similar trials but there are some differences that give it a much better chance of widespread success. The first is the mobile smartphone which has become part of the developed world's infrastructure and is rapidly becoming part of the entire world's infrastructure. The mobile phone will act as a bridge from present-day AR to AR of the future, particularly as mobile phones continue to grow in speed and capability. By continuing to use the hybrid tracking and sensor fusion techniques available in mobiles today, many of the challenges of recognition will be overcome and in turn create an environment where more and more interesting and useful content is created for AR.

In Chapter 3 we'll explore in much greater detail the potential uses for AR but it suffices today that Augmented Reality has the potential to impact almost every industry, from education to maintenance, medicine to business, entertainment to law enforcement.

SUMMARY

In this chapter we have defined Augmented Reality as the combining of real and virtual information that is interactive in real time and operates in a 3D environment. We've explored the history of AR beginning in 1962 and followed its development up to present-day. We learned about the differences between Augmented Reality, Virtual Reality, and quick response codes and explored many of the challenges and opportunities associated with AR.

In the upcoming chapters we'll explore in greater detail how Augmented Reality works, how AR will have the potential to affect and enhance almost every industry and the current and longer-term trends that are carrying augmented reality into the future.

The Types of Augmented Reality

INFORMATION IN THIS CHAPTER:

- How Augmented Reality Works
- Augmented Reality Methods
- Augmented Reality Methods
- Interaction in AR Applications

HOW AUGMENTED REALITY WORKS

In Chapter 1 we covered the basics of what augmented reality is and is not. In this chapter we will build on that information and start digging a little deeper into the technology to learn about all the pieces that make augmented reality work. We will discuss the necessary components that make up the whole process work and the different types of platforms used for augmented reality.

As we outlined in Chapter 1, the list below gives the core components needed for both fixed and mobile environments:

Hardware:

- a computer of some form factor, either a PC or a mobile device
- a monitor or display screen
- a camera
- tracking and sensing systems (GPS, compass, accelerometer)
- a network infrastructure
- a marker

Software:

- an app or program running locally
- Web services
- a content server

AR Systems and Functionality

Augmented reality systems can be divided into two basic categories: mobile and fixed. A mobile system gives the user just that, mobility, allowing someone to use augmented reality and move about freely in most environments. Fixed systems are naturally the opposite and cannot be moved but must be used wherever they are set up. A useful mobile or fixed system should allow the user to focus on the AR application rather than the device itself making the experience more natural and socially acceptable for the user.

AR Functions

The functions of augmented reality can be categorized in two primary ways:

1. The augmented perception of reality.
2. The creation of an artificial environment.

The differences between these types of AR are that each satisfies a different objective. In short, one is practical, one is imaginary. The first type of AR shows us reality and enhances what we can see and do, the second type shows what isn't real allowing us to see the imaginary. The AR interface makes the impossible possible. In this section we will explore some variations of these environments and how they fall under one of these two categories.

The Augmented Perception of Reality

Perception as defined by Webster's Dictionary is: a mental image, or the awareness of the elements of environment through physical sensation. augmented reality is at its core a tool designed to enhance the user's perception of the surrounding environment. In some cases it may be for purely entertainment purposes but one of the real useful functions of AR is to assist in the decision-making process. An augmented perception of reality is meant to provide useful information that will allow for a better understanding of our surroundings and improve our decisions and actions Figure 2.1 The next four figures, Figures 2.2–2.5, illustrate and describe some of the other variations that augmented reality is used for when augmenting the perception of reality.

The Creation of an Artificial Environment

The second category of AR functionality is the creation of an artificial environment. While the first category enabled objects or relations to be perceived in AR, the creation of an artificial environment uses AR to move beyond the creation of mental images to a level that allows us to see things that do not exist in the real world and

FIGURE 2.1 An Example of an Augmented Perception of Reality Where Relevant Information is Displayed to Aid in Decision Making

FIGURE 2.2 Depicts: Reality with Augmented Understanding Which Involves Making a Real Scene More Understandable by Providing Additional Information About the Scene with Virtual Titles and Symbols

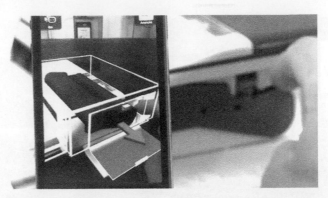

FIGURE 2.3 Depicts: Reality with Augmented Visibility Which Allows an Object to be Highlighted, Such as with a Wire Frame Model, so it can be Better Seen and Understood

FIGURE 2.4 Depicts: Perceptual Association of the Real and Virtual. This Occurs When a Virtual Object is Added to a Real Scene Either by Being Overlaid on Top of a Scene or Integrated in with a Scene

to share this view with others. Figures 2.6–2.9 illustrate and describe real and virtual environments that could exist, the real and virtual that no longer exist, environments that are beyond reality and impossible realities.

The Basic Process of Augmenting Reality

The steps involved with augmenting reality follow similar processes regardless if it is marker or location based. Marker-based AR is essentially embedding a 3D virtual model into a physical object while location-based AR follows much the same process but rather than identifying a marker, it assigns digital information to a set of grid

FIGURE 2.5 Depicts: Substituting the Real with the Virtual. With this Method a Digital Model Replaces a Real Object that Would or Could be Part of the Real Scene. The Digital Model is Often Positioned to be Viewed from the Same Point of View as the Real Object

FIGURE 2.6 Depicts: Associating the Real and the Virtual that Could Exist. This Involves Creating an Environment that Could Exist by Combining the Real and the Virtual. In this Example a Young Girl "Try's Out" a Digital Handbag to Decide if it is Something She'd Like to Have in the Real World

coordinates. The following steps, and Figure 2.10, outline the basic process for the creation of marker-based augmented reality:

- *Step 1:* Begins with the camera showing a live video feed.
- *Step 2:* The video stream from the camera digitizes the image and identifies the marker via border detection and the creation of binary encoded patterns.

FIGURE 2.7 Depicts: Associating the Real with the Virtual that no Longer Exists. AR can be Used to Blend Virtual Objects that No Longer Exist with an Existing Environment or to Associate Real Objects with an Environment that No Longer Exists. In this Example We See a Virtual Dinosaur Blended in with a Present-Day Forest

FIGURE 2.8 Depicts: An Environment that is Beyond Reality. This Function of AR Creates an Environment that Cannot Really Exist Simply for Artistic or Entertainment Purposes. In this Example Virtual Fighters are Blended with the Real-World Environment and the Combat is Further Emphasized with Visual Flares to Indicate Contact

- *Step 3:* The marker is identified the AR program positions and orients the 3D object in reference to the marker. It then orients the digital content with the physical marker.
- *Step 4:* The marker symbol inside the marker is matched with the digital content to which it is assigned.

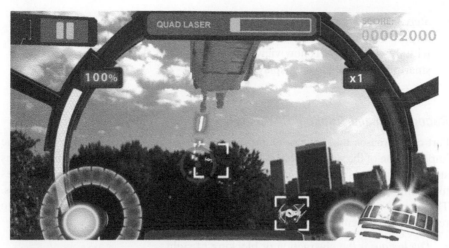

FIGURE 2.9 Depicts: The Impossible Reality Which is Often Used for Augmented Reality Games. In this Example Star Wars is the Theme for this Space Combat Game

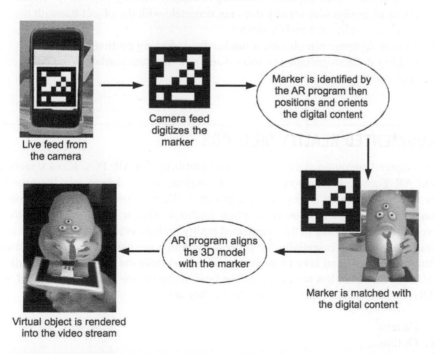

FIGURE 2.10 The Process for the Creation of Augmented Reality

- *Step 5:* The program aligns the 3D model with the marker.
- *Step 6:* The virtual object is now rendered into the frame and the video stream, with the AR content is now viewable on the display device, either a monitor, smartphone, or heads-up display.

Recognition and Tracking Challenges

Part of the reason the recognition problem is one of AR's biggest challenges is the imperfection of the real world in contrast to a lab or test environment. While this has steadily improved over the years, computers still have threshold limits when it comes to distinguishing background and foreground images in less than ideal conditions. There are a number of tracking challenges, listed and defined below, which lead to recognition problems:

- *Occlusion:* is the obstruction or blocking of sight.
- *Unfocused camera:* an unfocused camera lens will cause the marker details to be interpreted with lower precision, which leads to errors in positioning of the virtual object or complete non-recognition of the marker.
- *Motion blur:* is the apparent streaking of rapidly moving objects. In AR the effect of motion blur usually does not originate with the object but with the camera, usually on a mobile device.
- *Uneven lighting:* can obscure a marker by darkening portions in shadow making it unrecognizable, or recognized as a different marker to the AR application.

AUGMENTED REALITY METHODS

In Chapter 1 we outlined the four common platforms for AR: PCs, Kiosks, mobiles, and AR glasses. In this section we will continue to dig deeper into the specifics by which augmented reality is made possible. We will look at the actual types of augmented reality based on recognition methods. This will provide you with the broadest understanding of the augmented reality options available to you. Remember that recognition is essentially the process by which the hardware and the software determine where and how to augment reality and different digital devices will use different methods. But regardless of the type of the device you use to interact with AR, it will use one of these four methods; they are:

1. Pattern.
2. Outline.
3. Location.
4. Surface.

Let us look at each one in turn.

Pattern

This type of augmented reality system performs simple pattern recognition on a basic shape or marker. When recognized the system replaces that area with a static or moving digital element which can be anything from a 3D model, an audio or video clip, or some other piece of information as shown in Figure 2.11. This method is most commonly used when interacting with AR using a PC and a Webcam and often the person is part of the augmented video feed.

Outline

The outline method of augmented reality is the process by which a part of the body is recognized, such as hands, face, or body and is then blended seamlessly with any digital element. With the outline method a person is able to interact with a 3D object using natural movements, such as picking up a virtual object with a real hand. The camera tracks the outline of a person's hand and adjusts the virtual object accordingly. The method is similar when tracking a face. When the AR software detects a face, it determines the position of various facial features, eyes, nose, mouth, and so on then uses those positions as reference points for overlaying digital objects on the face. Once the software has recognized the face, it can also adjust for movement, redrawing the virtual objects in real time. An example of this is shown in Figure 2.12 where I'm using the Total Immersion program called Magic Mirror to try on a pair of virtual sunglasses that adjust as I turn my head. Figure 2.13 shows an example of an augmented reality Website promoting the movie "Transformers" which allows you to wear a virtual Optimus Prime mask.

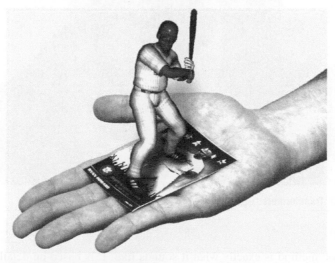

FIGURE 2.11 Marker-Based Augmented Reality

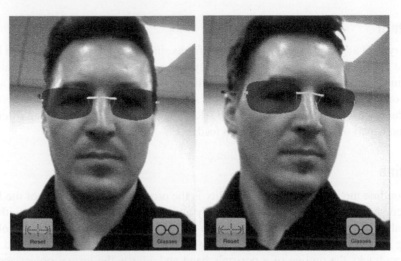

FIGURE 2.12 Augmented Sunglasses

FIGURE 2.13 Transformers "Optimus Prime" Augmented Reality Promotion

Location

The location method is exactly what it sounds like. It is based on detailed GPS or triangulation location information. Using this information and the position view of the camera the AR system can precisely overlay icons and virtual objects over buildings or people as you move around in the real world. Location AR is often used is through a mobile device. Modern mobile phones have all the necessary components to enable location-based augmented reality packed into one device: a camera, a screen, GPS capabilities, accelerometers, and a digital compass. There are a number of applications that run on mobile phones and create a personal window for merging digital information with the real world. They are called AR browsers. Much like Internet browsers that let you find information on the Internet, AR browsers let you find information in the real world. AR browsers are designed to allow you to see information about almost anything you point your mobile's camera at. A common example is the location of a coffee shop that may not be within your direct line of sight but is only a couple of minutes walk away or a review for a restaurant you are standing in front of. This information is "attached" to the specific GPS coordinates of interest points around you and displays the information on your mobile, in real time (see Figure 2.14). AR browsers also have channels, which are thousands of pieces of independently created content, and fold them into the application for everyone to access. Channels are often created based on as particular interest, such as popular restaurants to the nearest dry cleaner, and they are as varied as they are numerous. Examples of AR browsers that utilize location methods are Layar, Wikitude, and Tagwhat.

AR browsers are also not just limited to location methods. Due to the portability and high-resolution camera of the mobile device, the AR browser is also capable of using Pattern and Outline methods such as identifying QR codes. For example, an advertisement with a QR code, once it is recognized by the AR browser, can provide you information about the product or point you in the direction of the nearest store where you can find it.

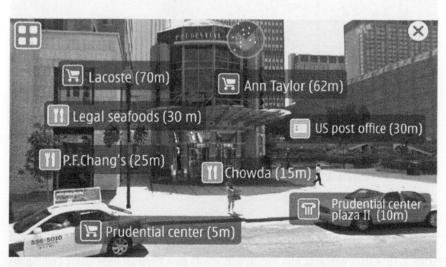

FIGURE 2.14 An AR Browser Showing Various Locations to the Viewer

Surface

Surface augmented reality is accomplished using screens, floors, or walls that respond to the touch of people or objects and provide them with virtual real-time information. In 2007 Microsoft released a coffee-table-sized computer called "Surface" which sees and responds to touch and real-world objects. In time this Surface computer was combined with augmented reality components and a project called LightSpace was created at Microsoft. LightSpace, combining surface computing and AR, creates an environment where any surface, and even the space between surfaces, is fully interactive (Figure 2.15). This combination of surface computing and augmented reality is called spatial computing.

LightSpace cameras and projectors are calibrated to 3D real-world coordinates, allowing for projection of graphics directly onto any surface visible by both camera and projector. In other words the entire room exists as both a physical and a virtual space at the same time. For example, after performing multi-touch interactions on a virtual object on the tabletop, the user may transfer the object to another display by simultaneously touching the object and the destination display. Or the user may "pick up" the object by sweeping it into their hand, see it sitting in their hand as they walk over to an interactive wall display, and "drop" the object onto the wall by touching it with their other hand.

The LightSpace program also has a cousin, called the Kinect. This motion sensing input device designed for the XBox game console lets users interact with a game through movements and voice commands rather than the traditional game controller. Since its release in 2010, the Kinect has been experimented with in a number of original ways. One recent development by a Kinect enthusiast was to develop an

FIGURE 2.15 A User Interacts with Virtual Documents on a Physical Desk Using LightSpace

FIGURE 2.16 An Augmented Reality Floor

AR-type platform that allowed any surface to be used as a computing interface. With this "depth camera" technology, cameras that are able to detect the ranges of physical objects and surfaces, becoming more common it is likely that this type of AR will continue to develop in some very interesting ways.

Another example of the surface method of augmented reality is the AR floor. The AR floor uses a special tile, which through the use of precisely calibrated vibrations can simulate pebbles, sand, snow, grass, and a variety of other surfaces (Figure 2.16). Sensors in the floor detect the force from a person's foot and then calibrate a response in the plate which when vibrated at the right frequency provides the simulated feel of different materials. Speakers inside the platform add the appropriate sounds, completing the illusion. In essence the floor becomes a large touch-sensitive screen. There is certainly potential for this type of technology for gaming, training, and entertainment. In time homes could be outfitted with this type of flooring to create the feel of any environment a person could want indoors.

AR DISPLAY TECHNOLOGY

There are generally three main types of augmented reality displays. They are:

1. Mobile handheld displays.
2. Video spatial displays and Spatial Augmented Reality.
3. Wearable displays.

In this section we'll explore the three types first and in the following section look at the methods by which we interact with AR.

Mobile Handheld Displays

Mobile Handheld Displays are best described by holding up a smart phone utilizing an AR app and seeing a digital image overlaid through the real-time viewer on the smartphone application. Devices like the Apple iPad, Motorola Zoom, and other tablets on the market are becoming popular for their form factor, ever-increasing functionality, and for AR which offers such larger display than the traditional smartphone (Figure 2.17).

Video Spatial Displays and Spatial Augmented Reality

Video spatial displays are utilized by holding up an AR marker to a Web camera which will then show the virtual overlay on a video screen or video monitor. Hallmark

FIGURE 2.17 Augmented Reality on an Apple iPhone and an iPad 2

is using AR equipped greeting cards through video spatial displays. The person that receives the card goes to a special Web site and holds the greeting card up to a Webcam. The person then looks at their computer monitor and sees a virtual image or video popup from the card with a birthday greeting or card message.

Toymakers are using video spatial displays to show their products to customer. Lego has created the "Lego Digital Box Kiosk" which uses the box itself as an AR marker to create a virtual display of what the completed set will look like (Figure 2.18). This is a great way for a customer to visualize their purchase.

Spatial Augmented Reality (SAR) displays use video-projectors, holograms, and other technologies to display digital information directly on to a physical object without requiring the user to carry the display (Figure 2.19). Spatial displays are useful because unlike most other AR systems which are small and personal, SAR takes the opposite approach and integrates the AR capabilities into the surrounding environment rather than with the user. This is useful if AR content needs to be seen by a large group such as in a university or museum setting. Spatial Augmented Reality also has the potential for being a useful tool for the design of control panels. Control panel components could be projected onto a physical mock-up giving designers and engineers a rapidly customizable view of their design. Taking this a step further it is also possible to include interactive tools designed to operate with the SAR thereby creating a fully functional prototype without having to install expensive, physical components.

FIGURE 2.18 The Lego Digital Box Kiosk

FIGURE 2.19 Sar Being Used to View the Engine and Transmission Components of a Car

FIGURE 2.20 An Artist Digitally Painting a Wall

Another use for SAR is digital painting or airbrushing. Similar to using SAR for control panel design, the airbrushing capability lets a designed "virtually" paint a physical object allowing designers to experiment with different colors and styles while providing a realistic preview of the finished product (see Figure 2.20).

Wearable Displays

A wearable display is a type of display that the user wears on their head like a pair of eyeglasses or goggles and is a type of head-mounted display (HMD), as shown in Figure 2.21. Wearable displays are also sometimes called video eyewear, video goggles, or personal media viewers. The design of a typical wearable display uses either one or two miniaturized video displays with lenses and semitransparent mirrors embedded in a helmet or eyeglasses. With continued advances in microelectronics many exciting new possibilities for head-mounted displays, specifically for collaborative visualization and AR applications, are being studied. Today HMDs are used for many applications covering a broad range of fields to include everything from flight simulation to engineering and design to education and training.

Video glasses are an HMD that acts as personal large screen monitor allowing users to experience augmented reality in a more natural fashion and with a larger field of view. Video glasses have been around since the late 1990s and unfortunately their performance has often trailed behind expectations, but this is changing rapidly and video glasses continue to improve while steadily dropping in cost. Vuzix is one such company that produces augmented reality glasses. With mobile phones now a permanent part of our technological infrastructure and the flood of quality online content that increases by orders of magnitude every year the time is fast approaching where quality, content, and price will intersect and create a huge market for wearable displays, as well as the content created for wearable displays (see Figure 2.22).

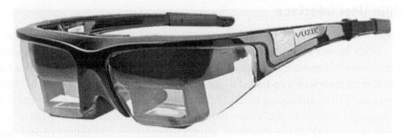

FIGURE 2.21 Vuzix Augmented Reality Glasses

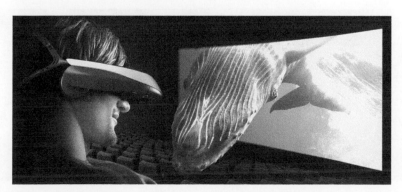

FIGURE 2.22 Video Glasses

Regardless of some of the drawbacks, HMD technology will offer a level of versatility that will make it useful on many levels across a wide range of applications. HMD technology will allow for the creation of Augmented Virtual Environments which will be robust computer-supported workspaces that give remote users a stronger, more real sense of "being there."

INTERACTION IN AR APPLICATIONS

Most augmented reality interaction happens visually on the personal level, at least today. Whether using a Webcam or a smartphone to access AR content, it is more often than not one person viewing data at a time. There are however other methods which we will cover in this section. They are the:

1. Tangible AR interface
2. Collaborative AR interface
3. Hybrid AR interface
4. Multimodal interface.

Tangible User Interface

The tangible user interface, or TUI, is a method used to further blend the real and virtual worlds by working to give a physical feel to digital information. Augmented reality provides an enhanced view of the world, but combined with the proper haptic (sense of touch) feedback, can take it to the next level by providing a powerful platform that allows the TUI to enhance a user's sense of physically interacting with virtual data.

An example of this is the Visuo-haptic interface created by the Magic Vision Lab. Their device, called the Phantom, allows users to see and touch virtual objects at the same location in space and time (Figure 2.23). The Phantom force feedback

FIGURE 2.23 The Phantom Visuo-Haptic Interface

pen can be used to draw onto virtual objects. In Figure 2.24 a digital bowl is attached to a physical base which the user holds along with the Phantom pen. This combination allows the user to feel like he is painting a real bowl in spite of the fact that the bowl is virtual. Force feedback devices are not the only means for creating useful TUIs.

Media X'tal, pronounced Media Crystal, creates a TUI by augmenting physical objects that are already meaningful to the user with additional information. For example, Media X'tal uses a hard plastic sphere as the generic prop then augments that object with a projection of a human skull which moves with the sphere on any axis (Figure 2.25) giving the user the physical and visual information simultaneously. This method of TUI can be applied to any number of shapes, such as cubes, spheres, or cylinders, whatever is suitable for the application needs.

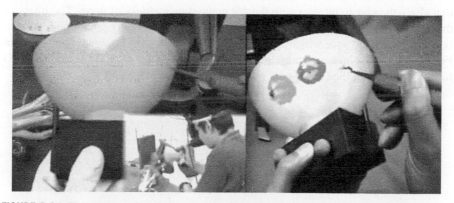

FIGURE 2.24 The Phantom Pen Being Used to "Paint" a Virtual Bowl

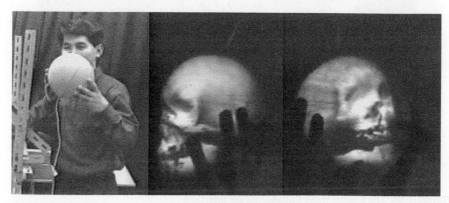

FIGURE 2.25 The Media X'tal Tangible User Interface

Collaborative AR Interface

Collaborative AR interfaces use a set of multiple displays to support remote sharing and interaction or co-located activities. An example of this type of collaboration is used in an AR system called Studierstube. The thoughts behind the design of Studierstube were to create an interface that "uses collaborative augmented reality to bridge multiple user interface dimensions: Multiple users, contexts, and locales as well as applications, 3D-windows, hosts, display platforms, and operating systems."

This type of collaborative AR interface can be integrated with medical applications for performing diagnostics, surgery, or equipment applications for design or routine maintenance (see Figure 2.26).

Hybrid AR Interface

Hybrid AR interfaces combine a number of different, but complementary interfaces that allow the user to interact with the AR content in a variety of ways. The intent of the hybrid interface is to provide a flexible platform for everyday interaction where it is not known in advance which type of interaction display or devices will be used. In Figure 2.27 an engineer is interacting with a digital helicopter model using an HMD for viewing and an iPad as a marker and control surface.

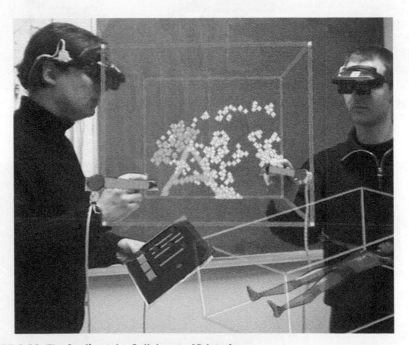

FIGURE 2.26 The Studierstube Collaborate AR Interface

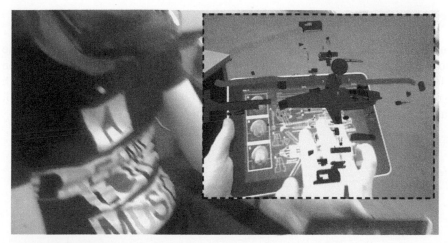

FIGURE 2.27 A Hybrid AR Interface

Multimodal AR Interfaces

Multimodal is defined as combining multiple methods of interacting with a system. The Multimodal AR interface interacts with real objects with naturally occurring forms of language and behaviors such as speech, touch, natural hand gestures, or gaze. An example of this is MIT's Sixth Sense which is also being called the "wearable gestural interface." Sixth Sense lets the user interact with information that is projected onto surfaces, walls, and other physical objects through hand gestures, arm movements, and in some cases blinking (Figure 2.28). The intent behind multimodal interfaces is to give users the flexibility to combine modalities or to switch from one input mode to another depending on the task or personal preference.

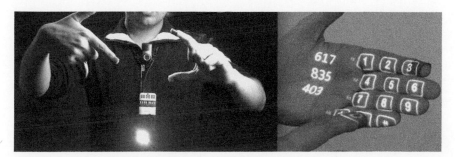

FIGURE 2.28 MIT's Sixth Sense Multimodal AR Interface

SUMMARY

In this chapter we looked at how augmented reality works giving a closer look at the components parts and process of creating AR. We examined the four most common platforms and the four most common AR methods. We concluded the chapter with a review of the different types of AR display technology. In the next chapter we will take a close look at all the uses and potential uses for augmented reality.

The Value of Augmented Reality

3

INFORMATION IN THIS CHAPTER:

- The Next User Interface
- Advancing Computer Interfaces
- The Uses of Augmented Reality

THE NEXT USER INTERFACE

Computer interfaces have come a long way over the past forty years. Starting from something arcane and foreign, early computers by their very lack of sophistication forced us to interact with them on their terms: assembly language, binary tape, punch cards, and so on. As time went on, monitors and screens gave users a real-time view of the command line and on until today. Augmented Reality has the potential to bring information to anything a person can look at and it is this capability that opens up incredible possibilities for the present and especially the future.

The Command Line Interface: The First Dimension

The first screen interface was the command line interface or CLI. This was essentially a one-dimensional computing interface where commands were typed in from left to right (Figure 3.1). Of course it was possible to work in two dimensions by moving down a line, but for contextual purposes let us agree to call the CLI a one-dimensional interface.

The Graphical User Interface: The Second Dimension

The next step was the graphical user interface or the GUI (pronounced: "Gooey"). The GUI is the digital personification of the *"paper paradigm."* The paper paradigm was conceptualized and created to make computers more user-friendly by making them resemble the non-digital workplace of the time; the metaphor used by most

```
Welcome to FreeDOS

CuteMouse v1.9.1 alpha 1 [FreeDOS]
Installed at PS/2 port
C:\>ver

FreeCom version 0.82 pl 3 XMS_Swap [Dec 10 2003 06:49:21]

C:\>dir
 Volume in drive C is FREEDOS_C95
 Volume Serial Number is 0E4F-19EB
 Directory of C:\

FDOS                <DIR>    08-26-04   6:23p
AUTOEXEC BAT          435    08-26-04   6:24p
BOOTSECT BIN          512    08-26-04   6:23p
COMMAND  COM       93,963    08-26-04   6:24p
CONFIG   SYS          801    08-26-04   6:24p
FDOSBOOT BIN          512    08-26-04   6:24p
KERNEL   SYS       45,815    04-17-04   9:19p
         6 file(s)         142,038 bytes
         1 dir(s)    1,064,517,632 bytes free

C:\>
```

FIGURE 3.1 A Typical Command Line Interface

modern computers and operating systems such as Windows, Mac OS, and Linux. The first computer to popularize the desktop metaphor over the earlier command line interface was the Apple Macintosh in 1984 and this metaphor remains ubiquitous in modern-day personal computing (Figure 3.2).

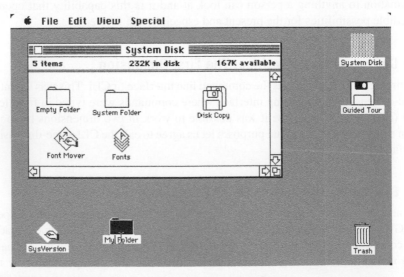

FIGURE 3.2 An Early Apple Macintosh Graphical User Interface

Augmented Reality: The Third Dimension

As we continue into the second decade of the 21st Century computing has continued to evolve becoming far more portable and powerful. As of late 2011 mobile phone usage has reached 5.9 billion subscribers worldwide, that's 87% of the current world population, and this trend shows no sign of slowing. Add to this the ease at which it is now possible to add "intelligence" to everyday objects through the use of cheap sensors, such as RFID chips and GPS, combined with powerful search engines that let us track both digital information and physical objects on the Internet. This convergence is changing the existing Internet into what is commonly being called the "Internet of Things" or IoT and Augmented Reality is a logical interface for this emerging IoT, allowing the physical world to become the backdrop, a desktop of sorts, for digital information as it created and moves around us.

Augmented Reality will not replace the older interfaces any time soon however, every interface current computing interface still in use provides a valuable functionality and while in some cases it may be limiting, in others it is ideal. As I work on this book I try to imagine how difficult it would be for me to go through the writing process using Augmented Reality. I expect I would find it to be a cumbersome experience since I am far more comfortable and efficient typing at a keyboard and navigating using a mouse. ViaVoice Gold is another good example of this. ViaVoice is a popular voice-to-text program that allows the user to speak what they want and have it typed out on the screen. While powerful, it can also require a great deal of practice to use effectively. Depending on the user it may simply be easier to type it out using the keyboard. As AR becomes more common there will still be a place for the command line and the graphical user interface for years to come since they will still be useful depending on the specific task needing to be performed.

In the next section we'll widen our view a little and look at some other advancing computer interfaces and how their development will likely impact the development and adoption of AR.

Mobile Browsing: Eliminating the Need for Searching

The Mobile Browser or AR Browser is a visual search engine that allows people to simply point their mobile device in a particular direction and see what it is they are looking for (Figures 3.3–3.5). This paradigm shift began with the "RWWW Browser" in 2001 which had the intent of aggregating functionality rather than separating it. They are still referred to as "browsers" because they provide access to web-based information similar to a traditional internet browser. In the previous section we described how the paper paradigm abstracted information stored on a computer to make it more familiar and more useful. The AR Browser takes this abstraction and functionality a step further and brings it into the real, three-dimensional world. Today the AR Browser is being used primarily to annotate objects and environments with public or private information. Taking into account the number of publicly available databases an AR Browser can draw upon, it is easy to see how useful this tool could be for almost any situation.

FIGURE 3.3 Wikitude AR Browser

Advancing Computer Interfaces

As computers continue to grow more powerful and their programming more flexible, we're seeing a variety of new and advanced computing interfaces that were considered science fiction twenty years ago. Two new interfaces that have really come to the forefront in the past five years are electronic paper and touch computing. Electronic paper and E-Ink technology have caught on rapidly and the popularity of the Kindle and the Nook e-readers only emphasizes the point (Figure 3.6). In 2011, for the first time, e-book sales topped hardcopy book sales stating clearly that electronic books are now poised to remain as a permanent fixture in the technology landscape. The other is touch computing. In 2007 Apple released the iPhone and Microsoft released the "Surface" tabletop computing, both allowed for a multi-touch and a multi-user experience (Figure 3.7). Capitalizing on the touch computing popularity Apple released the iPad a few years later which according to Bernstein Research was the fastest selling device of all time as of 2010. Additionally gesture-based interfaces are becoming more and more commonplace, such as the Wii and its revolutionary controller system and more recently the Kinect.

In the future continued improvement in touch, gesture, and voice technology will make these methods the standard for how we communicate with our digital devices. Building on this momentum, and using existing cheap sensor technology, such as RFID chip, these interfaces will be integrated into almost every area of our lives. With the convergence of sensor technology that allows virtually any object to become "smart" and the continuing growth of the "Internet of Things."

FIGURE 3.4 Layar AR Browser

While the topic of evolving interfaces could occupy a whole separate book, this trend outlines the exciting potential for Augmented Reality as just another one of the advanced interfaces we as computer users will have available to us.

Minority Report and Mezzanine

One of the most common examples used when describing AR is the iconic interface used by Tom Cruise in the 2002 movie "Minority Report." At the time of the movie's release the large gesture screen was an inspiring and plausible vision of what the future of computing would look like. Interestingly enough the interface in the movie is real. It is called the Mezzanine and was created by Oblong Industries (Figure 3.8).

FIGURE 3.5 Junaio AR Browser

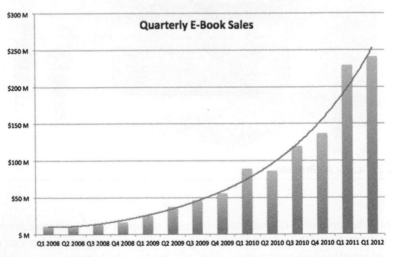

FIGURE 3.6 e-Book sales

Mezzanine was designed as a spatial operating environment meant to be used in conference rooms and other large meeting areas. The idea is to get people in a room together in order to synthesize information in the most collaborative way imaginable. In many ways it's like the Wii for business use, similar in function only much more accurate and functional. The goal of Oblong Industries for Mezzanine is to change how people work together.

FIGURE 3.7 The Microsoft Surface Table

FIGURE 3.8 Minority Report Touch Interface and the Mezzanine

Augmented Reality LEAP

The LEAP is a new gesture-based interface which is being advertised as "cheaper, smaller, more powerful, and more accurate then the Kinect." The LEAP is plugged into a computer through a standard USB port and needs no gloves or special equipment to use and can distinguish finger movements and tracking to 1/100th of a millimeter (Figure 3.9). The LEAP is taking aim at one of the biggest criticisms

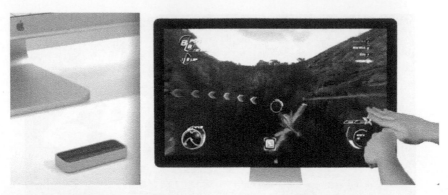

FIGURE 3.9 Leap Motion Interface

of Augmented Reality in smartphone and tablet devices which is that the user has to hold up the device to see augmented images.

Combined with augmented glasses, such as mounting a LEAP on the top of the glasses, it could create a hands-free way to see augmented visuals in a Heads-Up Display. The user would not need to hold up a tablet or smartphone to interact with the AR display. LEAP hopes to overcome the barriers of current technology by creating the interface that is manipulated with hand and finger movements.

THE USES OF AUGMENTED REALITY

AR will be used in a wide variety of ways. In this next section we'll break those uses down into five broad categories:

1. Sports, Gaming, and Entertainment.
2. Education and Maintenance.
3. Medicine.
4. Business.
5. Public Service, Law Enforcement, and Military.

For the remainder of this chapter we'll be focusing on the first four categories. Chapter Four will focus entirely on Public Service, Law Enforcement and the Military.

SPORTS, GAMING, AND ENTERTAINMENT

One of the biggest impacts that Augmented Reality has made is in the entertainment industry. How do we define entertainment? Entertainment, in its most basic definition, is a type of stimulation that amuses and gets one away from ordinary life. It is essentially a break from reality. It provides enjoyment, which is relative to the individual who is experiencing it. Different forms of entertainment include games, arts, and culture, movies, and music to name a few. Augmented Reality has the ability to transform every type of entertainment into a modern-day, cutting-edge experience.

Sports

AR has become common in sports telecasting. The yellow "first down" line seen in television broadcasts of American football games shows the line the offensive team must cross to receive a first down using the first and ten system. The real-world elements are the football field and players, and the virtual element is the yellow line, which augment the image in real time. Similarly, in ice hockey an AR-colored trail shows location and direction of the puck. Sections of Rugby fields and cricket pitches display sponsored images. Swimming telecasts often add a line across the lanes (Figure 3.10) to indicate the position of the current record holder as a race proceeds to allow viewers to compare the current race to the best performance.

Another example of Augmented Reality being used for sports includes an Augmented Reality app where, in celebration of the New York Giants Super Bowl XLVI victory, fans of the football team can create and share images of themselves wearing any of the Giants' 4 Super Bowl rings or pose with the Lombardi trophy (Figure 3.11). Sports gambling is also taking advantage of Augmented Reality. A company called Betfair is developing a mobile Augmented Reality application that would allow fans to place bets from their phones (Figure 3.12).

Gaming

The gaming industry is a multi-billion dollar global business that grows each year. As new technology emerges and is adopted it's not long before the gaming industry

FIGURE 3.10 Augmented Reality Being used in an Olympic Swim Competition

FIGURE 3.11 AR Super Bowl Trophy and Ring

FIGURE 3.12 The Betfair AR app

moves to take advantage of it and Augmented Reality is no different. One of the newest examples can be seen in Sony's new mobile gaming platform the PS Vita. The PS Vita is a mobile social networking game platform that has incorporated Augmented Reality into the device where players can initiate a game wherever they happen to be and use their current surroundings to allow for a more immersive gaming experience (see Figures 3.13 and 3.14).

AR and Location Information

A company called SimpleGeo creates tools that allow for location-aware applications. It has also built a software development kit that allows app developers to add AR features to their applications. This type of application has the potential to completely

FIGURE 3.13 The PSVita Console

alter the world of gaming and take it off the couch and out of the house into the outside world. Currently gaming startup companies are using this SDK to add weather data, demographic information, population density, and census data to alter the gameplay experience.

AR and The Kinect

The Kinect is a motion sensing, controller-free input gaming device by Microsoft that responds to human movements and voice commands, with the Kinect "you are the controller" as shown in Figure 3.15. Since its launch in late 2010, researchers and developers have spent a great deal of time experimenting with and hacking the Kinect.

The Kinect uses infrared light sensors that transmit invisible light at the objects in front of it. The object reflects the light back to the Kinect where its software encodes the results to determine the distance and movement of those objects. As a person stands in front of the Kinect, their body, arm, and leg movements are scanned by its infrared sensors. The technology is extremely accurate on the movement and distance of the person in the devices field of view.

The Kinect will be useful for AR development thanks to its embedded video cameras. The Kinect contains two separate cameras used for processing visual information and translating the visual data into digital information. This combination of the video streams from these two cameras allows a sort of 3D vision needed for determining what is "alive" in its field of vision and what is not, and for determining the distance live people are from the Kinect, giving the device its own depth perception.

Algorithms built into the Kinect device allow the device to use these two video streams to create skeleton joint data delivered from the controller to whatever application uses it. An application programmer can then augment the player's environment by either placing 2D or 3D objects over the display. Already people

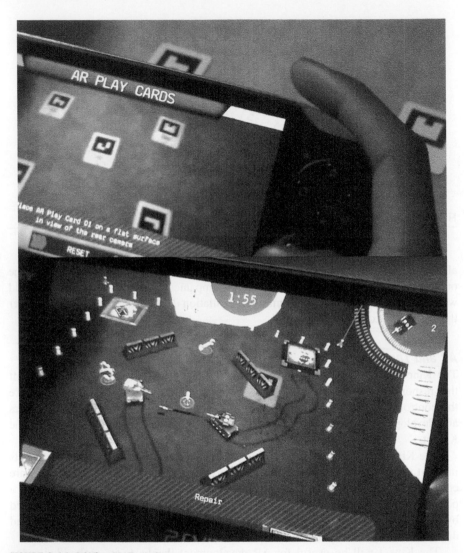

FIGURE 3.14 PSVita AR Tank Game

are experimenting with the Kinect and Augmented Reality. In Figure 3.16 two AR enthusiasts have created a bobble-head effect.

Holograms and 3D Video Conferencing

Holograms and 3D video conferencing are other areas that will explode with the use of Augmented Reality. If you are a fan of Star Trek: The Next Generation you'll certainly remember the "Holodeck." The Holodeck was a virtual reality simulator

FIGURE 3.15 The Kinect in Use

that the crew of the Enterprise would use for entertainment and training. A Holodeck participant would go into this simulator and interact and visualize a synthetic world that gave the illusion that they were in a tangible live environment that had real

FIGURE 3.16 Creating a Bobble-Head Effect with the Kinect

FIGURE 3.17 Zugara AR Interaction Interface

people and real interactions. Life-like holograms of simulated people would talk and physically interact. In no way do we think the Holodeck will be used anytime in the near future but the foundations of hologram interactions are getting closer to being mainstreamed with Augmented Reality.

One company that has taken a first step down this road is Zugara. Zugara, at the time of this writing, is developing a streaming Augmented Reality program that combines AR with live video conferencing for real-time interactive communication. Parents traveling can interact with their children and play interactive games in real-time. Doctors on opposite sides of the world can review a medical scan together. Students will be able to interact with detailed 3D models at their own pace to help understand the teachers lecture (Figure 3.17).

Other researchers and enthusiasts have also altered the Kinect to utilize this infrared technology to create three-dimensional video recordings of a person or object. It is reported that the accuracy regarding width and height is within 3 millimeters and in 1 centimeter in height. They have found ways to alter the Kinect, so that not only can it scan an object in the Kinect's field of view but also record it as video file while maintaining the 3D qualities of the recording. This has huge implications when we start to introduce Augmented Reality to the equation.

Once recorded, these 3D videos can then be attached to an Augmented Reality marker creating a hologram effect. Eventually when Augmented Reality glasses or contact lenses become mainstream we'll see more amazing uses of AR holograms. In time people may be able to have the sensation of touch with the holograms they interact with. Today researchers are working on utilizing sound waves to simulate the sensation of touch. Experiments with holograms and Augmented Reality have made some interesting discoveries and we'll probably see some major strides forward in the next few years.

AR and Virtual Worlds

In the days before the digital revolution and video games, children would go outside and play cops and robbers now kids meet up online and play Halo or Call of Duty. Shortly after the networked video game grew popular the virtual world emerged and became a new medium for a new generation. These virtual worlds have overwhelmingly attracted the young with less than 5% of the 800 million people (using 2009 numbers) in virtual worlds being over the age of 25. A total of $1.38 Billion was invested in 87 virtual goods-related companies worldwide in 2009 a 300+% jump from the $408 million investment in 2008. At the end of 2009 the total registered accounts in the virtual worlds sector reached $803 million and the Second Life economy totaled $567 million US dollars in 2009—65% growth over 2008. Virtual goods ranging from real estate to a bottle of champagne, traded just in the United States, are projected to be worth up to $5 Billion by 2015. This trend indicates that the blending of real-world stores and virtual worlds seems very profitable. According to Build-A-Bear Workshop in data released from a recent survey, one out of three guests who visited the virtual world store has also visited a physical Build-A-Bear store.

This type of virtual technology and the intelligent interaction between people and IT devices will enable new ways of doing things while creating new business possibilities. Over 1400 businesses, government organizations, and agencies have used Second Life to hold meetings, conduct training, and prototype new technologies since 2003. Add to this that game servers provide data for planet-size worlds, with details drilling down to a single leaf and blade of grass. Simply put, this means the amount of 3D content available online now exceeds what can be explored in a single person's lifetime.

Based on this information and the clear momentum that virtual worlds have gained it is not difficult to imagine the regular use of Augmented Reality to blend the physical world with the virtual world (Figure 3.18). In time, with a high enough resolution and seamless feel could give a person a real sense of physical connection even though it is with a digital avatar.

AR Facade is an experiment developed at Georgia Institute of Technology that, like the Second Life example, allows real participants to interact with a virtual married couple while moving freely inside a physical apartment. The virtual couple's life-sized avatars are viewed with a head-mounted display and allow the real people to engage in a conversation with the virtual husband and wife, using natural speech and gestures (Figure 3.19).

Ambient telepresence is another technique of blending physical worlds with virtual ones by creating telepresence connections between loosely linked spaces. These connections allow users to overlay several physical and virtual scenes and populate them with physical or virtual characters. An example of this is the Virtual

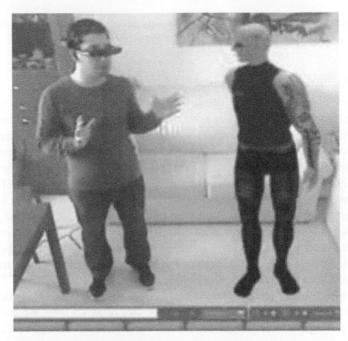

FIGURE 3.18 Augmented Reality Combined with Second Life

FIGURE 3.19 The Monitor Displays The Virtual Avatar the User Sees in the Head-Mounted Display While Interacting with AR Facade

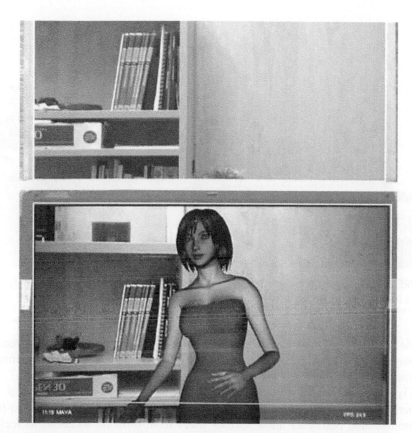

FIGURE 3.20 An example of a Virtual Mirror. The Top Portion of the Picture Shows The Reflection of the Room, the Bottom Portion Shows the Same Room with the Avatar Added to the Scene

Mirror interface. The intent behind this idea is to offer an alternative indirect solution for the visualization of 3D avatars rather than using head-mounted displays. This prototype allows a digital avatar to be added to what is perceived by the viewer as a mirror's reflection providing the feel of having a virtual person in a physical living space (Figure 3.20). The virtual mirror system contains one or more wall-mounted monitors that will also double as "mirrors" thanks to the small camera in the monitor. Each monitor will show the interior of the room as well as the viewer at which point the avatar will be rendered into the scene. The remote avatar will be added in such a way that they appear as part of the reflection in the mirror viewed by the real person in the room. In other words, these virtual roommates or visitors can only be seen as reflections in the mirror but never in direct view.

This method of telepresence has some big advantages in that a mirror is already a very familiar object having been used by people for centuries. The display is

FIGURE 3.21 The HyperMirror Interface. In this Image the Woman on the Left is the Only One In the Physical Room,the Woman on the Right is at a Different Location

subtle and unobtrusive in comparison to the current state of the art of head-mounted displays. Additionally it is an easy system to configure and reconfigure by simply moving the virtual mirror to the room of the users choice.

HyperMirror is another example similar to the Virtual Mirror, however the HyperMirror is a video conversation system that is not meant to simulate face-to-face communication but rather allow various users from different locations to feel as though they are all in the same room (Figure 3.21).

As the boundaries between real and virtual worlds continue to blur, it is very likely that people will start living part of their lives, or alternate lives, in a virtual environment. As advances continue with miniaturization, tracking, and head-mounted display devices people will have the ability to "insert" themselves into other people's virtual environments and vice-versa, meaning 3D digital avatars will move and interact in the real world.

AR and Social Networking

In 1971 the first Email was sent...the two computers were sitting right next to one another, but digital social networking was born. From this humble beginning the BBS (Bulletin Board Systems) was created allowing people to exchange data with each other over the phone lines. Then came USENT, Geocities, Friendster, MySpace, Facebook, and Twitter. It's a progression that is here to stay and will continue to evolve.

AR Flash Mob

On April 24, 2012 Amsterdam hosted the World's first AR flash mob. A flash mob is a group of people who assemble suddenly at a specific place, perform an unusual or artistic act, and then disperse. In the case of the AR flash mob, people in Amsterdam showed up to a specific point to have their picture taken with a digital "human statue." People with iPhones and Android devices, running the right AR software, could pose with a variety of characters ranging from Darth Vader to Superman (see Figure 3.22).

Mobile Social Networking

As social networking passed from the 20th to the 21st Century, the mobile phone began to grow more sophisticated on a yearly basis. Convergence of technology incorporated functions and features that went far beyond making simple phone calls and the mobile phone became a platform for social networking. Mobile social networks takes advantage of mobile communications (voice, texting, and MMS) and location-based services inherent in most mobile devices today. The next dimension is the inclusion of Augmented Reality (Figure 3.23).

An example of this is an app called "Augmented ID" which is a concept by TAT— The Astonishing Tribe. With a mobile device Augmented ID enables you to discover selected information about people around you as depicted in Figure 3.24. This has great potential for all users to control their own augmented appearance, by selecting the content and social network links they want to show to others.

Facial Recognition

Facial recognition is the method by which a computer identifies a person from a digital image or video. A face, from the perspective of an AR program, is nothing more than a unique marker and the potential uses for facial recognition combined with Augmented Reality are already being explored. Naturally this combination creates a new and powerful ability for people to be identified. Some critics argue that the harnessing of Facebook profiles, for example, can become an easy way to create

FIGURE 3.22 AR Flash Mob

FIGURE 3.23 Relationship Status Displayed in AR

FIGURE 3.24 The Augmented ID AR app

a massive identity database to locate and find information on participants of social networking sites.

Recognizr

Recognizr is a program created by Polar Rose that is able to detect a subject's face and then creates a unique signature by combining measurements of facial features and building a 3D model (Figure 3.25). This type of facial recognition capability can be used for a lot of different purposes, not all of them good. For that reason, the company designed Recognizr as a strictly opt-in service and people have to upload a photo and profile of themselves then associate that profile with different social networks before anyone can use the service to identify them.

Social Camera

Viewdle is a company that has created a product called "Social Camera." Social Camera combines Augmented Reality, facial recognition, and social networking using Viewdle's advanced face recognition technology to identify the people you take photos of the most, and tag them for you (Figure 3.26).

Movies

The movie industry in the United States is a 10 billion dollar a year business and information technology is now an integral and inseparable part of the production process. As Augmented Reality, and more specifically AR glasses, improve and become

FIGURE 3.25 The Regonizr Program

FIGURE 3.26 Viewdle's Social Camera Interface

more and more commonplace it almost a certainty the movie industry will make use of them.

The "Outernet"

Some groups are creating virtual reality games that incorporate Augmented Reality into the game. A recent reality game by 13th Street Universal called "The Witness" kicked off in Berlin in 2010 (Figure 3.27). The game chose numerous locations all over Berlin then had contestants traverse the city like a coordinated scavenger hunt. The participants begin at a pre-established starting point that then leads them to the rest of the locations and telling the story along the way.

Once the smartphone had found the marker, a video played showing a woman in danger who has been kidnapped by the Russian mob (Figure 3.28). At this point a series of clues are given, and utilizing an AR equipped smartphone, the player follows the clues and investigates the disappearance. By designing the story around Augmented Reality the player in effect becomes a part of the movie, and not simply a passive viewer, with the ability to affect the outcome. Based on skill, or lack of skill, the participant can either get to the finish line and save the kidnapped girl, or get double-crossed by one of the characters in the game.

An interesting side effect of this concept is that it could also be used to train people on how to conduct themselves in real-life situations. Detectives could get trained using AR simulation games allowing them to really feel the experience of what it is like conduct an investigation. Depending on how Augmented Reality movies are accepted by the marketplace it's easy to envision a whole new type of movie experience far beyond the choice of either a 2D and 3D version of a movies that are offered in theaters today. In the future viewers may not only have the choice of simply watching a movie in 2D or 3D but also going for the immersive, and certainly far more physically demanding, version of the movie in an AR environment.

FIGURE 3.27 The Witness AR Movie

FIGURE 3.28 A Player Interacts with a Character in "The Witness"

Virtual Sets

A virtual set is a construct that merges real actors with virtual backgrounds, in real time and in 3D (Figure 3.29). These types of sets have been around for some time and have left the studio and can now be purchased for home use for a few hundred dollars.

The ALIVE project from the MIT Media Lab is taking this concept a bit further by creating a smart room environment which allows for unrestricted

FIGURE 3.29 A Common Virtual Set

interaction with a virtual environment. They've even populated the environment with intelligent virtual creatures that respond to user actions. As devices such as the Kinect continue to improve and smart room environments become easier to create in everyday spaces, the idea of large-scale AR interaction will become more and more commonplace. Perhaps within the next ten years people will be able to put on a pair of AR glasses, walk into their backyard and see, and interact with, photorealistic dinosaurs.

Augmented Television

Imagine bringing this experience of an AR movie like "The Witness" into your living room. With augmented television you will be able to interact with, become part of, and control the story. Immersion in interactive stories is not new, but with the application of AR and using devices such as the Kinect, it will definitely create a new type of entertainment experience becoming a blend of storyline, motion picture special effects, and interactive video games.

The MetaMirror

A company called Notion Design has created a conceptual piece of Augmented Reality software that could make watching television an interactive experience. The MetaMirror tool is designed to mix live television and Augmented Reality (Figure 3.30). For example, the MetaMirror will be able to tell you the ingredients being used on a cooking show, the prices of your favorite football team's jerseys, and much more.

FIGURE 3.30 MetaMirror

Travel

People travel for a variety of reasons, to see new places, experience new cultures, to challenge themselves, to have fun, and for every other reason in between. Augmented Reality will play a part in future travel expanding the travelers' experience in exciting and useful ways.

Language Translation

Traveling in a country where you don't speak the language can be a daunting experience...especially if the new language is visually and phonetically different than your native tongue. Fortunately there is an AR tool called "Word Lens" that translates printed words from one language to another, in real time, using the video camera that is built into most smartphones (Figure 3.31). Additionally the tool does not require Internet access for translation, which is nice if you're somewhere that has little or no coverage.

Directions

When traveling it's often given that you don't know where you're going as well as you would back home. Today using a smartphone with a mobile browser can help simplify the navigation process and allow you to enjoy your trip without worrying that you'll get lost or won't be able to find something. Data on hotels, restaurants, shop offers, landmarks, social gaming, even menu translations, is at your fingertips (Figure 3.32).

FIGURE 3.31 WordLens Real Time Translation

FIGURE 3.32 Directions Using a Mobile Browser

An Expanded Experience

Along with directions and language translation, Augmented Reality will allow the traveler to have a much broader experience in their immediate surroundings more easily than ever before. While it's certainly valuable to tag digital information to a spectacular restaurant or a famous museum, there are also less obvious uses. AR has the potential to tell tales, enhance culture, and create incredible learning opportunities by retelling stories from present day and tales from long ago. Augmented Reality will also take geotagging to a new level by bringing geotags into the visual realm. For example, people could annotate key points in a particular environment, say a mountain trail, hat could be useful to other hikers and tourists that will visit in the future.

Augmented History

AR technology can play a very important role in learning history. Layers of digital history can be overlaid through the use of AR at a specific location. Imagine standing at the foot of the Statute of Liberty and utilizing your AR smartphone or wearing your future AR glasses. Maybe you wish to visualize the construction of the Statute of Liberty and utilize the "construction time period" which is a specific layer within the AR app. You will be able to see the phases of construction before your eyes with a digital image overlay or even video clip (if it exists). Perhaps you choose the time period when the Statue of Liberty was not even built but was a military fort. Numerous overlays could capture different time periods creating a wealth of knowledge for the user.

HistoryPin

HistoryPin is a program that allows you to experience places around the world at distinct moments in the past through your smartphone or tablet and see layers of historical photos superimposed upon wherever you happen to be (Figure 3.33). According to HistoryPin's CEO, Nick Stanhope, the project "aims to make billions of pieces of historical material the subject of mass-participation—to allow everyone to see the world through the amazing lens it provides."

More than 20,000 users have already geotagged over 50,000 pieces of content on the site, including photos, videos, audio, and written commentary.

FIGURE 3.33 HistoryPin Overlaying the "V-J Day in Times Square" Photograph on Present Day Times Square

FIGURE 3.34 Tagwhat

TagWhat

TagWhat is an entertainment app that has historic information on topics broken down into areas such as: art, food, nature, heritage, music, sports, and movies. For example, if you select "movies" TagWhat would display all movie-related events in your immediate area (Figure 3.34). The apps viewfinder shows your location and "blips" in your vicinity. Each blip represents a unique movie event that has happened and moving closer to a specific blip brings up additional information. For example let's imagine you are in downtown New York City using your TagWhat app looking for movie-related information. A blip appears and a "Carlito's Way" box starring Al Pacino flashes on the screen. Touching the blip on your screen brings up a description of the movie, along with the main actors and information about nearby locations where filming occurred. If you press the map button, it will locate the exact spot the movie was filmed and giving directions to the site along with a clip showing the scene that was filmed at that particular location.

EDUCATION

Education is second only to healthcare in terms of total spending in the United States with a combined education spending total of $1.6 trillion in 2011. The potential for Augmented Reality to influence and improve education is tremendous from creating simulations to conducting "virtual research" by allowing people to look inside areas that may not otherwise be accessible due to restricted location, such as inside an engine block or even inside a running engine. Augmented Reality will add a new dimension to learning in many ways. One simple example might be learning a foreign language, by giving the student the ability to walk around a familiar environment such as their house or neighborhood while having an AR program identify and describe an object in the language that person is trying to learn gives them a stronger memory bond. This method is known as "pegging" and it's a memory technique that allows people to associate new information to something they already know.

Augmented Reality Books

Augmented Reality can breathe new life into old books, and even new e-books, by augmenting specific content with 3D graphics or animations, audio or visual information as depicted in Figure 3.35. AR could be used in a traditional, hardcopy book where the fundamental information may not change a great deal but updates and advances could be viewed as AR in the appropriate section of the book and allowing an interaction with the content in a more engaging way.

FIGURE 3.35 Augmented Reality Used in a Traditional Book

Collaborative Learning

Expanding on the massively multiplayer online game (MMO) model and the blending of virtual world avatars into real environments, Augmented Reality will allow for an immersive, social, creative, gaming quality experience. This environment will create a huge LEAP forward in collaborative learning. Participants will be exposed to traditional task-based learning as well as learning opportunities and activities tied to a specific location. This, combined with a social networking element, has the potential to create an immersive, learning game-like environment as well as enhancing face-to-face and remote collaboration in whole new ways (Figure 3.36).

Construct3D

Construct3D is a three-dimensional, collaborative construction tool designed for mathematics and geometry education. The big advantage with this system is that students actually see the three-dimensional objects in 3D space, whereas previously they had to calculate and construct the same objects using traditional 2D methods. The Augmented Reality component gives the students an almost tangible picture of the complex three dimensional objects and scenes and as a result enhances and enriches the mental images that students form (see Figure 3.37).

The Augmented Reality Education Group

The Vuzix Corporation has created an Augmented Reality Education Group dedicated to developing a library of Augmented Reality training titles and topics available both for "off-the-shelf" use and customization. The library will include content that is applicable to:

- Medical professionals and medical diagnostics and procedures.
- Scientific research, analysis, and development.
- Academic instruction, research, and collaboration.
- Corporate Research & Development activities.

FIGURE 3.36 An Example of AR Collaboration

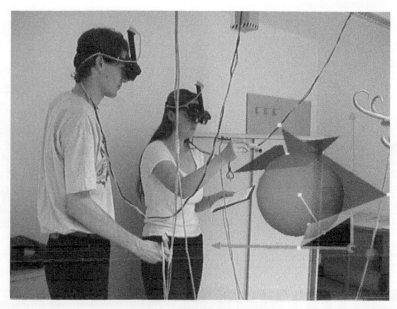

FIGURE 3.37 Two Students Using Construct3D

The Vuzix AR Education group wants to be the first stop for locating, publishing, and sharing ground-breaking research and industry advances while leveraging the evolution in training and communication that Augmented Reality makes possible.

MAINTENANCE AND REPAIR

With the benefits that Augmented Reality brings to education we only have to look a little farther to see how AR can be used for performing maintenance procedures on...just about anything. One prominent example of this is the Augmented Reality for Maintenance and Repair (ARMAR) program that was created by Steve Henderson and Steven Feiner at Columbia University. ARMAR explored the use of AR to help mechanics speed up maintenance tasks and repairs. The main objective was to illustrate that computer graphics, overlaid on the actual equipment to be maintained, would improve the productivity, accuracy, and safety of maintenance personnel (Figure 3.38). Using head-mounted displays the mechanics saw an augmented view of the machine they were working on with component labels and guided steps for maintenance. The mechanics were able to locate and start tasks more quickly, in some cases nearly twice as fast as they normally would without the aid of AR. A follow-up survey showed that the mechanics found the Augmented Reality condition intuitive and satisfying. Augmented Reality is being used more and more for all

FIGURE 3.38 The ARMAR System

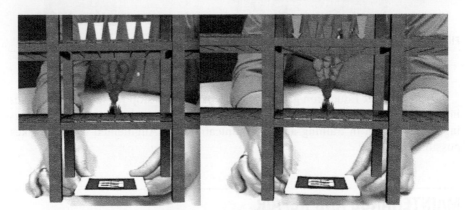

FIGURE 3.39 An AR Process Illustrating a Collapse Prevention Mechanism

types of maintenance and repair functions. While mechanical repair will likely lead the way, it is also being used to outline building collapse mechanisms (Figure 3.39) as well as other structural repair processes.

Augmented Manuals

Today user guides and repair manuals are digitally available online. In time, guides and manuals may be converted to become interactive instruction sets in Augmented Reality. Augmented manuals would be easier to understand if they moved beyond text and pictures to 3D drawings superimposed upon the actual equipment and providing step-by-step instructions (Figure 3.40). An example of this that exists today

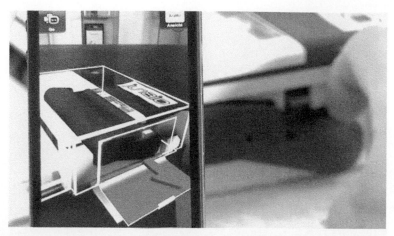

FIGURE 3.40 An AR Manual Giving Step-by-Step Instruction on How to Change the Ink Cartridge in a Printer

is a laser printer maintenance application also built by Steven Feiner's group at Columbia University.

MEDICINE

One of the most exciting potentials for Augmented Reality is in the field of medicine. With all of the capabilities of modern medicine there are still some features that doctors and surgeons can detect with the naked eye that they cannot see with an MRI or CAT scan and vice versa. This type of information, combined with the ever-growing number of medical sensors, can be combined and rendered, in real time and overlaid on a real patient. In effect, Augmented Reality would provide the doctor an "X-ray vision" look inside the patient, only instead of the sharp black and white, the full spectrum of colors would be available.

Augmented Reality also offers tremendous potential for new, minimally invasive surgery techniques. A surgeon could enter an operating room and see the patient as they are on the table, then using a head-mounted display the doctor could effectively look "into" the body of the patient, layer by layer, starting with skin, then muscles, moving all the way down to the bones (Figure 3.41). With this new perspective of the patient, the surgeon could then start the operation and only have to make a small opening in the body where tools such as an endoscope or catheter could be inserted into the patient. A head-mounted display would then augment the surgeon's vision showing where to operate as well as providing a virtual depiction of where other instruments and sensors may be located in the body of the patient as well, giving the doctor a digital "overview" of the patient as well as the area being operated on. Presently this scenario is still more dream than reality, but work is being done

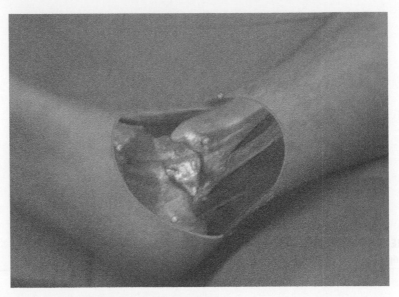

FIGURE 3.41 AR Being Used to Look into the Body

with Augmented Reality as well as new and smaller sensor technology to make this possible.

Following the thought of minimally invasive surgery, AR could be used to identify organs and other specific locations that may be important to avoid. In short, AR can be used to help doctors NOT to touch something that could hurt their patient. At UNC Chapel Hill, a research group has conducted trial runs of scanning the womb of a pregnant woman with an ultrasound sensor, generating a three Dimensional representation of the fetus inside the womb, and displaying it in a head-mounted display.

Gesture and voice commands are also starting to be used for surgical procedures. One example of this has come from researchers and surgeons from King's College London and Guy's and St Thomas' NHS Foundation Trust who are piloting "touchless" technology in the operating room. This process involves a computer program that takes a 3D image of a patient's anatomy and produces several 2D images taken from different angles and allows the surgeons to view, control, and manipulate medical images without physical contact through the use of Kinect technology. This allows the surgeons to maintain a completely sterile environment as well as relying less on assistants to manipulate the visual aid equipment for them, cutting down on miscommunications and errors (see Figure 3.42).

Medical schools could also benefit from Augmented Reality applications which would allow the student to see and conceptualize parts of human anatomy in a way that has not been possible before (Figure 3.43 and Figure 3.44) and virtual instructions could remind a novice surgeon of the required steps, without the need to look away from a patient to consult a manual.

FIGURE 3.42 Surgeon Using "Touchless" Technology in the Operating Room

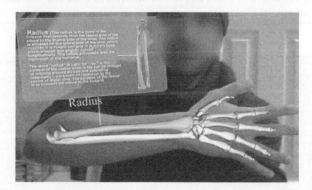

FIGURE 3.43 A Medical Student Using Ar to Visualize and Learn About his Own Skeletal Structure

Another innovative use for AR is to cure certain phobias. Using an exposure therapy program patients receive a treatment for cockroach phobia (Figure 3.45). The study, which tested the AR system on six people over 3, 6, and 12-month periods, demonstrated that it was effective in treating a cockroach phobia as all participants improved significantly after treatment.

Augmented Reality medial aids also do not have to be strictly visual. With the explosive growth of smartphones, iPads, and other touchscreen devices there recently has been a concerted effort to ensure that the visually impaired can take advantage of such technologies. An example of this is the smartphone app called "Navatar" which is designed to make it easier for the blind to navigate their way around buildings (Figure 3.46).

Navatar is being developed by Kostas Bekris and Eelke Folmer of the Computer Science Engineering Human–Computer Interaction Lab at University of Nevada, Reno. The system uses basic 2D architectural maps of a building or area and

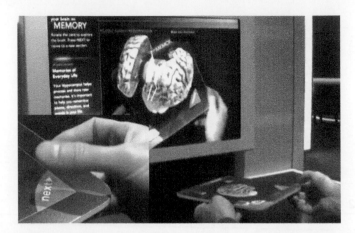

FIGURE 3.44 An Interactive Ar Kiosk that Allows Students to Look into And Examine the Brain from any Angle

FIGURE 3.45 The Cockroach Phobia Treatment Allows Patients to Visualize their Phobia

combined with the GPS, compass and accelerometer, functions found in most smartphones to detect and let the user know they have entered a specific building. Since the system has been developed for the visually impaired, the app can be thought of as using "auditory AR" by reading out the instructions in much the same way a car navigation system does today.

FIGURE 3.46 The Navatar System in Action

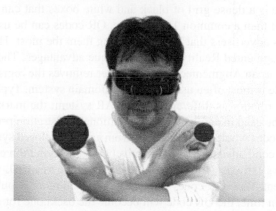

FIGURE 3.47 AR Dieting

Researchers are also envisioning ways in which AR can be used to improve a person's general health. One interesting example is the concept of an approach to dieting that uses Augmented Reality to trick the mind into thinking it is eating more food than is actually being consumed. The idea is that if the person sees an augmented view of their portion to be larger than it is, say 10 times bigger, the mind will believe it is full much sooner and that it does not need anymore food. In time it will be interesting to see how these types of AR experiences affect the mind and body and whether the results are positive and long lasting (see Figure 3.47).

BUSINESS AND COMMERCE

We have explored a variety of ways Augmented Reality can be useful to people in almost any situation. Naturally the underpinnings of most of these activities are commerce. Along with entertainment, education and medical uses AR is also being aggressively used in the creation and maintenance of business as well as maintaining or gaining market share.

Advertising, Public Relations, and Marketing

According to Business Insider, General Motors spent 4.2 billion dollars on advertising in 2010. Ford spent $3.9 Billion. Other companies such as WalMart, Verizon, and AT&T all spent at least 2.5 billion EACH just on advertising. In total these five companies spent 16 billion dollars on advertising expenses in 2010. With that kind of money as a sample figure it is easy to see how Augmented Reality will play a huge part in the future of advertising.

QR Codes and AR

A QR code, or Quick Response code, is a more sophisticated version of a bar code. The 2D QR code is a dense grid of black and white boxes that can hold 100 times more information than a common 1D bar code. QR codes can be used for a variety of things but it is advertisers that have been using them the most. However, pairing QR codes and Augmented Reality has some unique advantages. The first being that using a QR code as an Augmented Reality marker removes the registration problem since the QR code is most often used in a public domain system. Typically registered (augmented) information is different for each AR system; the markers used in one system may not be used in another without additional registration procedures. Using established QR codes would allow AR to go from a private, closed system to a public, open one. The second advantage is the relatively large information capacity of a QR code which allows extra data to be stored in the code, such as a URL which is hosting augmented content. With QR codes becoming more and more popular worldwide it is possible that, in time, the QR code will become the backbone for a public domain Augmented Reality system which moves beyond basic tracking and advertising to other areas such as social networking and security (see Figure 3.48).

FIGURE 3.48 A QR Code and Augmented Reality Combined for Social Networking

Billboards and Posters

Domino's has unveiled Augmented Reality billboards in the UK (Figure 3.49) that allow you to order straight from the billboard with your mobile. Consumers can scan the posters, placed over 6,000 sites and communicating a special "555" deal, with their smartphone, download a mobile ordering app and become a Facebook fan, all while standing at the bus-stop or walking down the street. The company worked with AR specialists Blippar to develop the technology which is now being used on a variety of items (Figure 3.50).

Movie Ads

In 2009, to advertise the upcoming reboot of the successful Star Trek series, the producers released an Augmented Reality advertisement called "Experience the Enterprise." The movie poster is the marker and once augmented gives the viewer the ability to tour the Enterprise as well as learn about the crew, fire the weapons, and go to warp speed (Figure 3.51).

Another successful advertising campaign became a viral video for Iron Man movies which depicted Augmented Reality glasses for everyday use similar to the heads-up display as seen in the movie. Unfortunately the technology that was

FIGURE 3.49 Domino's AR Billboard

FIGURE 3.50 Blippar providing a Recipe that Uses Ketchup

FIGURE 3.51 The "Experience the Enterprise" AR advertisement

portrayed in the video was a fabrication, however something like this may be a reality sooner rather than later. And with this example as a model it's highly likely we'll see something like this in the near future.

Car Ads

Much like movie advertisements, automakers have used AR to create ads that allow the user to "see" and interact with a car in a virtual showroom environment. Figure 3.35 depicts an AR ad for a Mini Cooper. Other car manufacturers, such as Mercedes-Benz, are starting to adopt AR as well to allow customers to design their cars virtually on the showroom floor (see Figure 3.52).

Retail and Shopping

Augmented Reality will transform the traditional shopping experience in years to come as personal customization and the social networking aspects of shopping are incorporated into the way we presently shop. One example of this is the EON Interactive Mirror that lets clothing stores provide virtual dressing rooms that will allow the customer to personalize an outfit in real time as well as give him or her the option of seeing the outfit in the context for which they are buying it. (Figure 3.53) For example, if a woman is shopping for a party dress not only will she be able to see what the dress looks like on her at that moment, in whatever color she chooses, but she will also be able to place herself at a representation of the party giving her the "feel" of being in a specific place and time while wearing the dress. Add to this a social networking element and now people will be able to shop virtually with one another even if they are on opposite sides of the world.

Another example of this type Augmented Reality in action is being used at Selfridges in London. Shoppers on the street are able to "try on" any watch they like without having to go into the store as shown in Figure 3.54.

FIGURE 3.52 Mini Cooper AR ad

FIGURE 3.53 The EON Interactive Mirror

FIGURE 3.54 Selfridges AR Wristwatch kiosk

Moosejaw

Moosejaw, a retail clothing company has released a new app that utilizes Augmented Reality in a unique way. Certain pages in the Moosejaw catalog act as an AR marker, which when scanned, give the illusion of using X-Ray vision to undress the catalog models down to their underwear. It's an interesting gimmick to draw attention to their products and raises some interesting questions on where AR in advertising may go in the future. It's an advertising maxim that "sex sells" and in May 2012 Moosejaw released a second AR app called the "Sweaty & Wet" App and Catalog. In this version the AR app allows the user to move a virtual water gun and spray the augmented model giving the appearance that the model is wearing a wet T-shirt. As AR continues to become more robust and more common, it will be interesting to see how the Moosejaw AR experiments will influence other apparel companies or even the adult pornography industry (see Figure 3.55).

Augmented Reality Windshields

AR is the key visualization component in the "Virtual Cable™" car navigation system which uses unique human–machine interface (HMI) and breakthrough 3D engine hardware providing a commercially available augmented windshield. The Virtual Cable system overlays a red digital line on the windshield providing the driver with a greater than line-of-sight view of the surrounding area.

Virtual lines and objects aid in navigation and scene understanding during poor visibility conditions, such in heavy rain or in fog. Figure 3.56 depicts the Virtual Cable system in action with the line extending out from the top of the windshield following the path of the road and bends sharply to the right indicating the direction

FIGURE 3.55 The Moosejaw "Sweaty and Wet" AR app

FIGURE 3.56 The Virtual Cable System Depicting a Virtual Line for the Driver to Follow

FIGURE 3.57 The Pioneer HUD panel

of the driver's next turn. This type of visual cue gives the driver a preview of what's ahead far beyond normal sight. Additionally Virtual Cable can be used for speed control, tailgating avoidance, points of interest alerts, alternate route presentation, collision avoidance, and off-road navigation.

Pioneer Stereo is also working on an AR system for cars that leverages the driver's smartphone and a HUD panel that resembles a transparent sun vizor (Figure 3.57). The system is designed to allow the driver to access different menu functions while viewing navigation cues and other vital statistics on display in the HUD. In time AR windshields may cease to be safety glass at all and could evolve into a reinforced metal television monitor with no inherent transparency, something like a tough, windshield sized iPad that pipes in the outside world through a series of video cameras for added protection and security.

SUMMARY

In this chapter we've explored the history and evolution of user interfaces as well as new computing interfaces that are changing the way people interact with their computers. We also looked at a wide range of uses for Augmented Reality. From entertainment and sports, medicine to education, Augmented Reality can be applied in a variety of innovative and useful ways by providing people with more information about a place or object or making something that is not easily seen visible. In the next chapter we will continue to explore the uses of Augmented Reality looking AR applications for public service and military uses.

The Value of Augmented Reality: Public Safety, The Military, and The Law

4

INFORMATION IN THIS CHAPTER:

- Public Safety, The Military, and The Law
- AR and Law Enforcement
- AR for Firefighters
- AR and the Military
- AR Satellite Finder
- AR Flight Tracker
- AR Ship Finder
- Augmented Reality and The Law

PUBLIC SAFETY, THE MILITARY, AND THE LAW

Augmented Reality has approached a technical maturity where we can now say it is present in our society and is now becoming a true presence in the modern world. Augmented Reality has enough infrastructure support to thrive. The mobile platform has helped Augmented Reality become widely distributed and begin a mainstream transition that will transform our world. AR will push innovation to new levels and create flexible and functional tools to help society. Tools can become double-edged swords that can be used for good and evil. We must also look at the downside of the technology to discern the unintended negative consequences, and perhaps prevent them. When the Wright Brothers took their first powered manned airplane flight in 1903 for 12 s did they think about the Stealth bomber? It is almost certain they did not. Did they think about an airplane used as a missile that could be flown into a New York City skyscraper? It is safe to say they did not. This chapter will delve into some of the clearly good and bad uses of AR. We will highlight how the public safety sector, military, and the legal field will be influenced by the use of Augmented Reality.

AR AND LAW ENFORCEMENT

Engineers at Frequentis have developed a program called iAPLS, which is a mobile extension of the firm's Automatic Personal Location System, which shows the location of officers using the GPS signals sent by their radios. If a suspect has a smartphone that police have a fix on, or a covert officer is closely following them, they too can be tracked. Officers can also use their phone to "tag" the location of a suspect package to make it visible to fellow law enforcers.

For police officers tracking targets via helicopter, Churchill Navigation of Boulder, Colorado, is augmenting live helicopter video with terrain-contoured street maps in real time (Figure 4.1). Without this, says founder Tom Churchill, it is hard for pilots looking at a maze of streets on screen to know which street a target is on. It works by tightly coupling the map database to the software that controls the camera's motion.

Tying databases of information to a specific location to provides rich, immediate understanding about that place and its history. With Augmented Reality, a law enforcement official can "see" behind bricks and doors, into target premises for possible dangers, hazards, and its history before going in. They can know what is behind the door, accessing a deep history of the premises, including past emergency calls, and much else.

FIGURE 4.1 An Augmented View from a Police Helicopter

This type of app recently underwent a successful 90-day trial with the police departments of San Mateo and Burlingame, California. It now is beginning to roll out to other agencies for implementation.

Drone Technology and AR

A drone is another name for an unmanned aerial vehicle, an aircraft that is operated without a human pilot on board. Drone technology can be an effective tool for surveillance, providing real-time data for law enforcement and the military. In the United State in February of 2012 Congress passed a bill allowing for the increased use of drone usage over US airspace and the Federal Aviation Administration (FAA) predicts that 30,000 drones could be in use over US airspace by the year 2020.

Drones coupled with Augmented Reality offer the potential for object recognition, license plate recognition, and a number of other possibilities for law enforcement—right down to the individual officer—and creating a sophisticated tracking system of people, objects, and vehicles. In addition to object recognition drone data feeds could identify suspicious movements in a crowd which might indicate a riot or potential terrorist movements (Figure 4.2).

Collaborative Crime Scene Investigation

Oytun Akman of the Delft University of Technology in the Netherlands is developing an augmented reality system that will allow local police to investigate crime scenes, remotely supported by expert colleagues through AR. The system also creates 3D videos of the scene for later review. The purpose of the system according to Akman is to "support collaborative spatial analysis between crime scene investigation on location and experts colleagues." Initial results show that this approach to remote

FIGURE 4.2 The View from a Drone as Law Enforcement Moves in During a Riot

spatial interaction with the physical scene enabled investigators to address issues on site in collaboration with experts at a distance.

AR FOR FIREFIGHTERS

There is tremendous potential for AR to have amazing benefits for emergency responders. Firefighters stand to gain incredible new advantages to battle blazes and save victims through the use of Augmented Reality. Companies such as Tanagram Partners are focusing on many different areas where AR could have a positive impact on society. One approach they are working on uses AR to give firefighters a better way to communicate with each other and navigate quickly in a high risk situation where they can swiftly find victims and identify the source of a fire.

One of the basic rules of responding to fires is to make every effort to keep your personnel out of unnecessary danger. Augmented Reality could be of great assistance to a Fire Chief in such high pressure situations. A fire department equipped with augmented reality glasses and helmets could immediately give the Fire Chief the lay-out of the surrounding power grid showing where to set up to avoid overhead electrical wires and telephone poles which could potentially melt from the heat of the fire. Next the Fire Chief and his crew could see a virtual view of the five nearest fire hydrants through their glasses. Once the firefighters are inside their AR, visors would help them navigate through the structure.

Firefighters always wear fire gloves when entering the burning building. They are bulky, heavy, and do not give the firefighter much flexibility to do delicate or intricate movements. AR overlays on their gloves give an even greater advantage because the simple movements of touching a finger to activate a radio, or a map are easy to accomplish (see Figures 4.3 and 4.4).

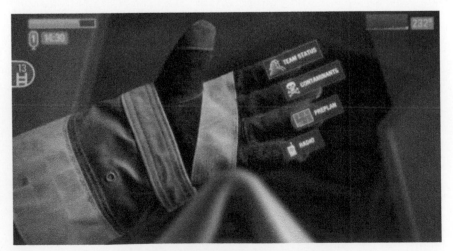

FIGURE 4.3 AR Visualization Shows a Firefighter Critical Visual Data

FIGURE 4.4 Shows the Live Data Feed that One Firefighter can See From Another Location or Through Another Firefighters Point of View

This type of AR technology can also easily apply it to other types of rescue situations. Urban Search and Rescue teams, paramedics, police officers, battlefield medics, and other response type units can greatly benefit from the power of AR.

AR AND THE MILITARY

Head-Up Displays (HUDs) and Helmet-Mounted Sights (HMS) have been used by the military for years. A chin turret in a helicopter gunship can be slaved to the pilot's HMS, so the pilot can aim the chin turret simply by looking at the target. Another example is the F-35 Lightning II which displays information in the pilot's helmet-mounted display, allowing the pilot to look through the aircraft's walls as if he was floating in space. Data or objects can also be projected onto transparent helmet-mounted displays for use in troop training exercises—allowing soldiers to carry out exercises in real landscapes augmented with depictions of enemy troops or tanks, for example. By using AR in this way, the Army can put soldiers through a wider range of scenarios than would normally be possible, without the need for extra hardware or manpower. Tanagram is currently developing military-grade augmented reality technology that—if developed to the full potential of its prototypes—will significantly change the way military combat is carried out (Figure 4.5).

One example of this is Battlefield Augmented Reality System (BARS). The system consists of a wearable computer, a wireless network system, and a see-through HMD. The system targets the augmentation of a battlefield scene with additional information about environmental infrastructure, but also about possible enemy ambushes. The system includes a visor that displays data in an officer's field of view.

FIGURE 4.5 Tanagram Concept of Battle AR

Information Dominance

"Information Dominance" is defined as the degree of information superiority that allows the possessor to use information systems and capabilities to achieve an operational advantage in a conflict or to control the situation in operations other than war while denying those capabilities to the adversary. Achieving information dominance is a constant goal for senior military leaders and AR technology has the potential to make that goal easier to achieve.

One example of where AR is being used for information dominance is the Persistent Close Air Support, or PCAS program whose goal is to give that controller the ability to "request and control near-instantaneous airborne fire support." The intent behind this system will be to reduce collateral damage and potential fratricide to friendly forces. The system is meant to give a single soldier on the ground a direct data link to the drone, or manned aircraft, circling above.

With further development and incorporating augmented reality glasses, the wearer could basically "see" all of the aircraft in the relative area—even if they are a hundred miles away. For example, a solider could look up in the sky and see an icon letting him know that there is a drone 30 miles out at 21,000 ft. It could also display what type of ordnance the plane was carrying, letting the soldier make a quick decision and determine if the drone would be appropriate for the mission.

In 2012, DARPA, the Defense Advanced Research Projects Agency, placed an order with Innovega for augmented reality contact lenses for use on the battlefield. The idea behind the lenses is that they will allow the wearer to focus on close and far-away objects at the same time allowing the solider to remain situationally aware while seeing images or video from satellites or drones (Figures 4.6 and 4.7).

FIGURE 4.6 Video Feed from a Military Drone

FIGURE 4.7 Concept View of the Drone Video Feed Looking Through the AR Contact Lenses

Another example, mentioned in the previous chapter, is the ARMES system, which was created for the US Marines. The test had six participants carry out 18 tasks using an AR system. For comparison, the same participants also used an untracked headset which only showed static text instructions and views without arrows or direction to components and a stationary computer screen with the same graphics and models used in the AR headset version of the system.

The mechanics using the AR system located and started repair tasks 56% faster, on average, than when wearing the untracked headset, and 47% faster than when using just a stationary computer screen.

AR SATELLITE FINDER

DishLoc is an augmented reality application that allows the user to view where geostationary satellites are located to include azimuth, elevation, and tilt for each satellite (Figure 4.8). This allows the user to adjust the dish position for optimum placement.

AR FLIGHT TRACKER

One of the greatest developments since the map has to be GPS (Global Positioning System). Navigation takes on a new perspective when Augmented Reality is blended into tracking transportation movements. New types of Augmented Reality Apps allow a smartphone user to track moving objects like airplanes or ships.

For aircraft there is an app called Plane Finder AR which combines beacon feeds transmitted from airborne aircraft, using a technology called Automatic Dependent Surveillance-Broadcast (ADS-B). Planes with this technology broadcast a beacon that other base stations can receive that identifies the plane name, type, altitude, heading, speed, and various important identifiers. The Plane Finder AR app can receive the signals from these beacons and show an augmented reality overlay with real-time identifiers of aircraft in your region (Figure 4.9).

Airport ground crews could identify ground aircraft easily with overlaid AR flight information Fueling trucks could receive live data feeds to receive real-time remaining fuel readings of an aircraft or any maintenance concerns, which could be shown over an app or AR glasses. Control tower personnel could see coordinates of incoming aircraft, view closed caption pilot radio transmissions via AR overlays, aircraft speed, heading, and other important aviation indicators for safe flying. Ground aircraft that

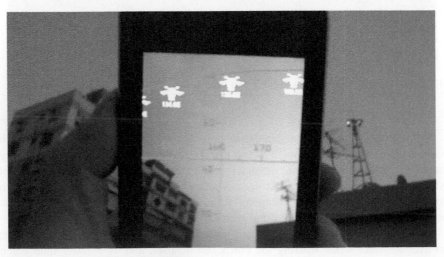

FIGURE 4.8 DishLoc AR Satellite Finder

FIGURE 4.9 The Plane Finder AR App

were not in safe portions of the tarmac could be highlighted in the color red through AR overlays on the tower's external windows to show a possible danger.

From an airport security level, unauthorized ground crew members could be flagged through AR overlays on security cameras, security booths, or through ground security personnel holding AR capable smartphones, tablets, or AR glasses.

Pilots could also benefit from AR overlays. Specially fitted aircraft could have AR overlays through the cockpit window that highlight the proper path to reach safe runways, or identify proper landing areas. If an airborne aircraft has an emergency, AR overlays could not only identify unoccupied runways but could also track ground traffic and identify safe (non-airport) landing options. Unoccupied highways or areas clear of high-tension wires or other obstacles may be quickly identified through smart computers and relay this information and overlay it over the cockpit windows. The possibilities are endless with the power of AR.

AR SHIP FINDER

Augmented Reality can be just as useful for tracking ships. One such app is called Ships Ahoy by Pinkfoot. Similar to aircraft, ships also have a navigation beacon. It is called Automatic Information System (AIS) and the purpose of the technology is to prevent vessel collisions that may be in close proximity (Figure 4.10).

Tugboat operators, Tender operators, or dock personnel could benefit from apps such as Ships Ahoy. Advanced AR overlays could also help operators guide a large ship into port. AR glasses or a tugboat AR window could digitally guide the operator and show the correct positioning or movement of the cruise ship into its intended docking spot.

FIGURE 4.10 The Ships Ahoy AR App

Augmented Reality along with modern navigational equipment could increase the number of ships and airplanes within a close proximity of each other and reduce flight delays and increase vessel volume in certain ports or congested areas. AR would create efficient systems and most likely reduce manpower for complicated tasks. It would allow for more precise movements and reduce the risk of loss of life and property damage.

AUGMENTED REALITY AND THE LAW

One of the murkiest areas about AR will be the legal issues that will develop and how the legal system adjusts to these changes. Legislators will have to weigh in on the impact that AR has on society and address the changing digital landscape with these new innovations. Brian Wassom Esq., legal expert and author of the Website, www.AugmentedLegality.com, has closely monitored emerging AR trends and how the legal system may be affected in years to come.

Brian predicts that the five biggest legal areas to watch are the following:

- Regulatory Requirements.
- Negligence.
- Copyright.
- Privacy.
- Discovery.

Regulatory Requirements

Although this area may seem mundane for the potential explosive impact of AR, it creates one of the greatest challenges for lawmakers. Implementing such change represents a huge challenge to keep users safe while not stifling innovation and another technology revolution. Brian believes that such real-time, high-resolution devices may require large signal bandwidth, which may need equipment with large battery capabilities. These batteries may pose a potential health hazard to the user or other areas where regulatory oversight is needed. High-tech electronic powered devices may require necessary regulation with these consumer electronics. Brian raises the issue of high broadband requirements and 4G mobile devices that may need additional regulatory requirements. How will these signals be emitted and at what risk to the user? High-powered eyewear may pose risks to the users. Will these types of signal transmitting have an impact on other devices? Congress and the Federal Communications Commission (FCC) will have to address these issues as AR gains more momentum.

Negligence

AugmentedLegality.com has addressed the issue on the many ways that AR games can get developers in trouble. A distracted viewer could wander off a curb or sidewalk and get injured, or follow a digital scavenger hunt only to get hurt wandering into an unsafe area. These types of issues may result in negligence lawsuits and costly litigation. Vehicle manufactures are working on AR windshields and some AR eyewear manufacturers are planning icon pop ups in the AR users' field of view. These types of distractions could lead to injury or severe harm to the user. Some moving AR icons or multi-images could disorient an AR user and lead to a Vertigo-type event or other disorientation. Lawsuits may lead to regulatory requirements or Terms of Use clauses while utilizing eyewear.

Copyright

This might be one of the most interesting areas in AR law. Brian stresses that many forms of intellectual property will be infringed on in AR space. This trend has been clearly demonstrated in virtual worlds where courts have addressed these virtual property issues. According to Brian, what makes copyright such a particular concern is that AR displays (images, video, digital models, and the like) will obscure the same real-world displays. This will create a large amount of difficulty for copyright owners to know that infringements are taking place because it will not be seen with the naked eye. Only someone who is part of the AR or digital view will be able to detect infringement. Many copyright owners already have difficulty going after violators who hide behind anonymous means out in cyberspace. Digital packages could be left behind without any trace to the original person that violated that copyright. Brian predicts that we will see a potpourri of copyrighted materials in virtual space.

It might not be unusual for entire physical environments to be completely obscured by virtual AR content. Replicated cartoon characters could linger around every corner for kids without permission of use from the copyright owner. Brian believes that the end result will "be a reconceptualization of what copyright protects. The Internet is already forcing that discussion; AR space may finally break the current copyright legal framework."

Privacy

Privacy might be one of the biggest areas of concerns when talking about the power of Augmented Reality and legal implications. People become concerned when "Big Brother" capabilities can identify a citizen without their knowledge and/or permission.

The ability of facial recognition coupled with Augmented Reality can create tremendous opportunities to reveal the identities of the general public. Freely available resources on the Internet already allow easily discoverable information on citizens. A company called Polar Rose, recently acquired by Apple, has been working on a beta mobile application that users can tie their numerous social networking sites to a digital image of themselves. This can allow strangers the opportunities to scan a stranger and be able to see Augmented digital overlays that show what social networking sites the person belongs to (Figure 4.11). Brian raises the issue that these new capabilities could create a new form of invasion of privacy and believes "the real privacy concern that is specific to AR is the ability to physically associate data with a person in real space." The possibility of knowing a person's home address floating over someone's head via a mobile app as you walk down the street creates serious privacy issues. We may see legislation and regulation controlling these types of relationships between personal data and the use of AR applications.

Discovery

Brian Wassom highlights that discovery may be a very practical problem that people may run into. When lawsuits are filed, there are questions on how lawyers will recreate what the person in AR space viewed. How will the viewers' imagery be recreated or replicated? Is there a legal duty that companies have to preserve the imagery that a person sees? These types of issues may have to be addressed as the AR field expands.

FIGURE 4.11 The Polar Rose AR Social Networking App

SUMMARY

In this chapter we described how the military, public safety, and the law can and will be impacted by Augmented Reality. We discussed how Augmented Reality can be used for good and bad and the need for law enforcement to pay attention to rapidly changing technology advances. Law enforcement can utilize AR in many positive ways and track sex offenders or identify repeat offenders. Digital trends are also making it easy for AR to be coupled with drone technology, facial recognition, and geo-location. Many new military uses of AR will continue to pave the way for innovation and technical sophistication. We discussed how AR apps can also track vehicles, ships, and aircraft like never seen before and in real-time. We also discussed the legal and social issues that AR brings to society. The legislature and courts will have to make important decisions on how to adjust current laws which also include privacy, constitutional rights, and safety.

Innovators and Organizations 5

INTRODUCTION

Since AR is still an emerging technology, we felt it would be useful to showcase some of the developers and organizations that are having a major impact on Augmented Reality. While researching this book we discovered numerous innovators, groups, and businesses that specialize in Augmented Reality worldwide. This chapter takes a closer look at some of those people and organizations.

Dr. Steven Feiner

In order for us to understand where AR is today we must take a look back at where Augmented Reality came from. There are numerous scientists, innovators, and dreamers that have brought AR to its current state of existence. We would be remiss if we did not mention some of the earliest contributors to Augmented Reality and the painstaking research and development that were undertaken. Dr. Steven Feiner, Professor of Computer Science at Columbia University, is one of the early scientists that began experimenting with Augmented Reality over 20 years ago. Dr. Feiner's research and development, through countless experiments and projects, has helped propel Augmented Reality and trained PhD candidates who would become instrumental in the progress of AR development.

Dr. Feiner defines Augmented Reality as the idea of augmenting the things that we experience in the real world with virtual material, doing it interactively in real time in a way that essentially geometrically registers the virtual material with the real material. Dr. Feiner is cognizant to carefully not express a strictly visual preference since AR does not have to be only overlaid graphics to an environment. Most groups tend to be visually and graphically oriented, but in the broader sense, one can experience audio AR, haptic (touch) AR, olfactory AR, and gustatory (taste) AR. Most of what he and his lab have done has been predominantly visual AR research. However, he believes it is important to step back and see Augmented Reality in the multimodal, multimedia experience as opposed to sole understanding that it is an added graphic in the real world.

Dr. Feiner started getting involved in AR in the latter part of 1990. Early in 1991, he worked on a project that involved creating a window manager that was designed to allow the user to supplement their view of a flat panel by using a head-mounted display. The project dealt with this limited space graphical window manager that could potentially block other things in the display since at that time, the user had a limited amount of display space to work with. The goal was to either bring the things you don't want to have blocked to the front or you could also make the things that you didn't care about smaller. What Dr. Feiner really wanted were large displays, but they weren't affordable during that time, so he looked for other options to work around this limitation. If he were to take a user's view of a conventional flat panel display, and create a wearable head-worn display tracker that was optically see-through, he could then overlay additional graphic objects on top of that flat panel display. Those additional graphics could be fed above and below and to the left and to the right of the window manager. The user then could see windows beyond the ones they would see on the actual flat panel itself. The head-worn display was not as high quality as the flat panel. At the time, Dr. Feiner wanted to do most of his work on the flat panel but the technology did not support high-quality resolution for head-worn displays. In the experiment, he could push things off the flat panel display, literally move them, in the case of the system he built, to grab hold of a window move it up and instead of it stopping at the edge. Then he could keep on moving the window off the flat panel because of the tracked head-worn display, which tracked the orientation of the head movements. This early 1991 experiment, in the case of this very first probe, would allow the user to see beyond the outline of the window with its name and actually see its contents. It was high resolution at the center, which is where the user did most of their work, to low resolution off to the sides. If the user looked beyond the flat panel, they could basically look all around and see many windows off on the sides. Traditionally when it comes to visual displays, the hierarchy of importance is the stuff that is seen right in front of you is more important. The things at your periphery are less important. Dr. Feiner understood that this concept has been talked about in both conventional media and computer-based medium. Through this experiment, he wanted to try to exploit an environment that could use a head-worn display to virtually represent all of this stuff that was in secondary and tertiary space. This was the very first AR system he built. After that, Dr. Feiner participated in many projects. One of his fondest projects was working on the first outdoor applications with AR. In 1986 he built a "rather clunky backpack (containing around 45 pounds worth of stuff) on an external frame backpack that was the first outdoor AR system." This was the first mobile AR system, it was called the "Touring Machine" shown in Figure 5.1. His research paper led to the 1997 paper titled "A Touring Machine: Prototyping 3D

FIGURE 5.1 The Touring Machine

Mobile Augmented Reality Systems for Exploring the Urban Environment—Steven Feiner, Blair MacIntyre, Tobias Hollerer and Anthony Webster." The main themes stressed in this work were:

- Presenting information about a real environment that is integrated into the 3D space of that environment.
- Supporting outdoor users as they moved about a relatively large space on foot.
- Combining multiple display and interaction technology to take advantage of their complementary capabilities.

One of the interesting questions put to Dr. Feiner has been the progress of Augmented Reality over his career. Having spent over 20 years working on Augmented Reality projects, experiments, and publishing numerous papers, the question posed was: has the research and development on Augmented Reality progressed to his expectations? Has it developed slower, faster, or rolled along in a consistent manner compared to his expectations? I guess the chuckle that came from Dr. Feiner was an obvious indicator that things never conform to our or his expectations. He believes that generally, scientists in academia tend to be overly ambitious on the technology that they are working on, in which he self-confesses that he is no exception to that. In the early 1990s, he had his own preconceived predictions of where AR would be in the year 2000; specifically of how the military maintenance and repair through Augmented Reality would work and become a modern-day norm. He thought this because he was building systems in the early 1990s that were functional concepts but not ready to be deployed en masse. As he explains, "The problem is that it is not just technology to be successful. You have to make the technology in enough quantity to make it affordable. You have to be able to sell it to people who want to wear it so it can't look like something that people would perceive as 'weird looking.' There is a whole bunch of barriers to something actually 'catching on.' Many of which were less technological ones and more business model ones." Dr. Feiner admits that he didn't understand those things back then, but now has the realization of how little he knew back then. He jokingly laughs that he probably still doesn't understand it to this day. He compares technology examples such as the Betamax vs. VHS as a prime example. Sometimes it is less about technology that makes a product better and more about the business model that drives it to success.

While he remains very excited about the recent developments in Augmented Reality he is a little "gun shy" on making concrete predictions, but expects some amazing things for the coming decade.

Another question posed to Dr. Feiner was this: *Will Augmented Reality change social culture or influence it?* Dr. Feiner believes we will see many different changes and points to the example of how mobile phones have changed social culture. Dr. Feiner points out that a person sitting on the subway listening to music off his cell phone would not be seen in the 1950s. It is not unusual for a person to stop midstream during a heated discussion to stop and go to a Google site to pull more data or information on a topic. These changes that we see with the mobile phone and the resulting social change will also be seen with other technologies such as Augmented Reality. There are a lot of things that change because of technology and here we are talking about a technology that might be there with you all the time. I am going to wear something that's not just listening to music but being able to look at and listen to media that is relevant to what I am looking at and listening to in the real world around me. That lets my system track, for example, my position and my orientation, overlays information about a person who is walking toward me reminding me who they are. It helps me as I walk down the street, not to have to pull a map out and look like a lost tourist, which is what I really am. Instead I'll be able to walk in the direction that I need to go to get to a restaurant that I have never been to before because small amounts of additional graphics and audio will appear and guide me. Dr. Feiner uses the example of Facebook where you can indicate your birthday on your page. Normally only a few close friends might know your birthday but with Facebook, all your friends can know your special day; and many of them send you birthday wishes, people who ordinarily would not have done so in your life years ago because readily available technology did not afford them that information. Now imagine if you could have a virtual persona, a virtual set of information, tied to you through facial recognition. You allow this virtual persona or virtual set of information be tied to your facial characteristics. You would allow the general public the ability to see this information if they scanned you with an AR capable device (utilizing facial recognition) that would see the identifiable information you made public. You may have a virtual birthday hat pop up on your head or a virtual button that pops up and asks people to "Ask me how old I am today." People would then greet you and wish you happy birthday if they had "Augmented Reality" capabilities with them. Soon many different people who had that technology and capability to see your publicly available information would greet you. Eventually you might consider it rude when a person greets you and does not wish you happy birthday. There becomes an expectation of another person's baseline technology capability that becomes societies' new norm.

Dr. Feiner sees himself continuing to be active in exploring AR research and benefiting from research funding in AR maintenance and repair. He credits the Office of Naval Research as one of the premier groups that has recognized the importance of AR research, which has funded some great projects. He hopes that continued funding, from all different groups, will make AR commonplace. He is hoping that 5 years from now there will be some very interesting head-worn display capabilities. Dr. Feiner is truly a research pioneer in Augmented Reality development and one of early innovators in Augmented Reality progress. He is an asset to Columbia University and will continue to make giant strides in this technology revolution.

Ori Inbar

I was fortunate enough to interview the mastermind of the organization, Ori Inbar, also CEO of Ogmento, an AR gaming start-up company. Ori's basic view of Augmented Reality is about overlaying graphics on real-world objects in a meaningful way in real time. As Ori explains, "The challenge is to understand what you are looking at, where you are, utilizing all your sensors to understand the world in a way never experienced before." Ori got into AR in 2007 when he realized that he didn't want to see his children inactive and sitting on the couch all the time. He always saw his children stuck in front of a computer screen or surfing the Internet, which prevented them from being active in the real world. This sedentary life was counterproductive for his kids, thus becoming glued to a traditional gaming system as many young children do today. He envisioned a way, by utilizing AR's incredible potential, his kids could experience an AR environment by getting off the couch and exploring the world in a fun gaming environment, while becoming mobile. He knew that the traditional things that attracted kids to the Internet and gaming world could be revolutionized through AR and become a more healthy interactive opportunity to stimulate kids' minds and bodies. Ori had heard of the scientific term "Augmented Reality" which seemed to be a hidden secret that was being explored in the lab environment for so long but had not transitioned to its true potential in the real world. His mission became to find a way to bring this technology to everyone. This concept pushed Ori to create the Augmented

Reality blog "Games Alfresco" which is still active and pushing the AR gaming concept while following his passion. The New York Times has described Ori's blog as "The leading Augmented Reality news blog." As Ori followed his passion, he became involved with a small group of AR enthusiasts, which formed an AR discussion group of other researchers, developers, and AR start-up companies. He used his blog as a springboard to discuss AR developments and work with other interested AR members. During this time the iPhone came out and Ori believed that the iPhone could become a saving grace for the future of AR. The AR members with Ori petitioned Apple to open their API (Application Programming Interface) for the iPhone camera to give AR developers the ability to create mobile AR applications. Although Apple never formally responded back, three months later Apple opened their API to create amazing AR opportunities. Wikitude and Layar took that opportunity to build their first AR app on the Apple platform. Although we will never know what influence Ori and his members had on Apple, the ability for Augmented Reality to flourish on the Apple platform is history.

In 2008 Ori attended the New York Tech Meet-up. This meeting showcased five presentations and demos on new innovative technology. Ori's experience at this meet-up gave him the idea to form the Augmented Reality of New York. The ARNY Meet-up soon gained momentum for Ori working with Chris Grayson, Tish Shute, Patrick O'Shaughnessey, and others to become a thriving place where AR researchers, start-up businesses, and interested AR members could discuss the advancements of Augmented Reality. ARNY was responsible for sparking meet-ups on AR from all over the world. This led Chris Grayson to founding the site ARmeetup.org that highlighted all AR Meet-ups around the world. We will talk more about ARmeetup.org when we discuss Chris Grayson in a later section.

ISMAR (International Symposium of Mixed and Augmented Reality) was a group that formed but focused more on the science of Augmented Reality. Ori recognized the importance of ISMAR, but wanted to create a new conference that focused on the industrial side of the business of Augmented Reality and not on the science. The birth of the Augmented Reality Event was born which started in 2010 in Santa Clara, California. The second annual event took place in 2011. The Augmented Reality Event (ARE) was the largest gathering of Augmented Reality professionals from all over the world. The purpose was to create an event to get AR professionals together to share ideas beyond the lab environment. Ori Inbar, Tish Shute, and William Hurley were the brainchildren behind the original concept of the Augmented Reality Event. It has now become the staple of AR professionals hosted in the United States.

When it comes to Ori's company Ogmento, the mission was to make games that would inspire kids and adults in an interactive live environment to leave their couches and computer chairs and experience AR in a mobile environment. Ogmento is one of the first start-up companies that focused on AR games in the world. Ogmento has developed games such as Paranormal Activity: Sanctuary, Put a Spell, Sketch AR, NBA: King of Court, and other AR mobile games. One of the most interesting things about these mobile AR games is that they are social interactive games where people can compete against each other or play these mobile AR games alone.

The Paranormal Activity app allows participants to walk down any street and cast a protective spell around their workplace or a location they frequently visit. They can team up with other mobile app players or compete against someone from around the world. In late May 2010, Ogmento secured $3.5 million in funding from Chart Venture Partners. Ogmento continues to thrive as a growing start-up company that has a very bright future.

What fascinates Ori is that Augmented Reality could make more capable as humans. One of Ori's favorite movies scenes takes place in the Matrix where Trinity uploads how to fly a helicopter in a few seconds after she sits down at the controls of a helicopter. The instant download of the flight instructions, training, and manual makes her an instant expert helicopter pilot. Although that type of Hollywood moment is far fetched, the ability for AR to make users smarter and create an almost instant expert is very possible. We will see amazing leaps in real-time intelligence through AR technology and the advancements are only limited to ones' imagination. Ori's favorite phrase about AR is that "Augmented Reality is a hack of the brain." It can take the brain to places like never before seen and its change will have far-reaching effects to our world like never seen before. It creates a leap in the ability of human-ity to do things. Many people may wonder how Ori Inbar got to the place he is now. Ori simply states that his "love of AR is a passion and the openness in collaboration is the key to its future success." This passion has fueled ARNY, GamesAlfresco, Augmented Reality Event, and Ogmento. The AR community is thankful that a small spark created a lifelong passion in him that has put the wheels in motion for an amazing technology and emerging AR medium.

Tish Shute

Tish Shute is another key person that has made important contributions to the world of Augmented Reality. Tish feels that Augmented Reality goes beyond the visual dazzle and augmentations that most people immediately think of when it comes to AR. It is a part of a wider movement of augmenting human intelligence and ubiquitous computing. Tish likes to think of Augmented Reality as, "reality that feels different rather than merely looking different." AR, she points out, it is part of a new world of human—machine intelligence that goes beyond merely visual accomplishments or qualities.

Tish got involved in Augmented Reality early in her career doing special effects for film and television. She worked on motion control photography, using robotic cameras to create perfectly registered layers of effects on film for Sci-Fi scenes. It was a natural transition for her, when powerful processing, ubiquitous networks, and smart phones emerged, to work on Augmented Reality for the real world.

UgoTrade is her personal "think tank" blog where she has some great dialogs with some fascinating innovators. She considers this a great way to create a think tank of "one" that can harness many different expert insights. Her approach creates the opportunity to examine the commonality and diversity of AR trends and develop-ments. Her blog also connects Augmented Reality with the concept of ubiquitous computing—a world where computing is no longer tied to laptops and desktops, and sensors are everywhere, such as the iPhone which already puts a number of sensors in your pocket all at once. The network is now permeating every nook and cranny of our society, and the world is becoming a digital platform for our daily lives. Tish's blog explores interesting aspects of this networked world that reaches far beyond the "end to end" Internet and the World Wide Web.

One of Tish's favorite quotes is by Alan Kay—"The best way to predict the future is to invent it." She believes that Augmented Reality and ubiquitous computing are exciting ways to explore this. Tish has been doing research and development with Will Wright's think tank Stupid Fun Club. Will Wright, a gaming industry legend, was the creator of The Sims, SimCity, and Spore, and many other innovative projects and highly successful games.

Tish was also very instrumental in creating the annual Augmented Reality Event, which has been held for the last 2 years in Santa Clara, CA. The 2011 event brought on Chris Grayson to join forces with Tish and Ori Inbar to organize the event. Keynote speakers and very influential innovators like: Bruce Sterling, Jaron Lanier, Blaise Agüera y Arcas, Frank Cooper, Vernor Vinge, and Will Wright were on hand bringing much excitement to the event. Tish considers Bruce Sterling as one of the "Prophets of AR" whose consistent presence at the past three ARE conferences has helped solidify its importance. Along with the other innovators, Tish also feels that tech pioneers and game design legends, Will Wright and Jessie Schell, two gaming innovators, propelled the event, and helped inspire game developers and legitimize the AR event. Tish also feels that early movers like Metaio, Layar, Ogmento, and Mobilizy with their early involvement with AR development on mobile smartphones were pivotal in giving momentum to the emergence of an AR industry. Mobilizy's app Wikitude was a very early example of an Augmented Reality mobile application. It showed Wikipedia tags overlaid in real time over the environment. Wikitude also opened up the opportunity for users to add to a database of shared Augmented Reality content.

Tish feels that "the future of AR is data-driven." AR is going beyond just having an image or simple text overlaid on a scene. It is becoming an interaction with the world based on real-time data. She points out the augmented experience is all about situational awareness and uses the project "Leafview" as an example. Leafview was developed by Dr. Sean White from Columbia University. The intent of the project was the creation of a digital collection of plant life specimens that users could access in the field through an AR view with hand-held or mobile devices. Leafview identifies over 90,000 plant specimens and allows researchers and laypersons to have a tremendous amount of research data at their fingertips out in the field and to be able to easily identify a specific plant species in real time.

Tish describes an increasingly data driven world where there is the potential not only to see the data flows like traffic and crime in a city from a bird's eye but we will also be able to see a single leaf and how it is connected to rest of the world. Many people are interested in making the enormous amount of data in the complex world we live in more accessible. AR is an important part of this because it can make data contextually relevant in the real world in real time at a place and time that it is most useful. As AR matures, it will, increasingly, become an integral part of our daily lives. What is interesting to Tish is the stories we will tell through data and how AR can make these stories more useful, intelligible, actionable, and fun. Augmented Reality and ubiquitous computing is creating a truly magical world where people and objects will have the potential to communicate in ways we have barely imagined.

Chris Grayson

When it comes to Augmented Reality, Chris Grayson defines it from a production centric definition because of his day job. He defines Augmented Reality as "special effects rendered in real time over real life." A self-described "Tech Junkie," Chris' influence came from his grandfather who worked for NASA, the FAA, and other organizations using cutting-edge technology in the early 1970s. Chris was partly influenced in the 1980s and 1990s, hooked on reading the cyberculture magazine "Mondo 2000" which covered topics such as virtual reality. Wired magazine spawned from the influence of Mondo 2000 and the cyberculture media. Chris reflects on a January 1994 edition of "Gadget World" tech magazine that had an article about a product called "Virtual Vision." The concept describes glasses with a video inset, that overlays an image in a real-time environment. This description of an Augmented Reality consumer grade product was some of the earliest exposures to influence Chris to the idea of Augmented Reality. Let us take a closer look on how Chris Grayson's path led him to influence the Augmented Reality world. The New York ARDevCamp was an event where Chris Grayson was first introduced to Ori Inbar and Tish Shute in 2009. That was where the seeds for the first Augmented Reality of New York (ARNY) Meet-up were started. Chris had noticed that during the New York ARDevCamp someone had turned their webcam on from their laptop and was streaming the event. Ori Inbar liked this concept and thought it was a good idea to live stream ARNY Meet-ups and Chris volunteered to do it since he had some experience. Chris liked the idea of how ARDevcamp had a Wiki set up and wanted to build upon the concept with a well-organized video platform to help people who were interested in learning and sharing about AR. That is how ARmeetup was born. Chris was able to harness other AR meet-ups and put them under one roof at the website. The website has forums where users can post comments and find archived meet-ups. ARmeet-up became a one-stop website that connected all AR meet-ups from other places: Los Angeles, Toronto, San Francisco, London, Manchester, Raleigh, Sydney, Chicago, and New Zealand. What was amazing about Chris Grayson's vision was that he streamed meetings live via UStream. Now any AR enthusiast in a remote part of the world can watch a meeting live as if they were present. This is a great resource for AR enthusiasts to see live or archived meetings. It is a great place to learn about the developments of AR enthusiasts from around the world. The goal of ARmeet-up was a simple platform for people of the different meet-up groups around the world to communicate and share the information. Chris works for a New York

City production company called Humble. They have been working on some projects that are incorporating AR and even aspects of facial recognition. Chris is founder of "Tedx Silicon Alley" which can be found easily with a basic Internet search. In 2011, Chris was named one of the 25 Most Influential People Tweeting about AR. This is the largest compilation of AR Twitter feeds in the world.

One of the most important technology parallel arguments that Chris makes is this: "Augmented Reality equals ARPA's original vision for the computer network." Well what does that mean? He makes the case that if we look back on how the Internet came to be; we see similar parallels between the formation of the Internet and the future path that Augmented Reality will take. Chris goes beyond just that principle alone, he feels that the vision of early innovators could finally be carried out via the pure potential that AR holds. Chris starts off his theory saying that if we look back at the history of the Internet, its original concept was not the World Wide Web and a slick Internet browser interface. Early scientific papers written about the Internet were conceptual and theoretically based. The graphical user interface had not been created, yet these innovators envisioned a network where all the world's information would be made immediately available to any particular person. They saw a future network that could be ubiquitous throughout the world. As the conceptual and theoretically views transformed into real hardware advances, programming and network successes, the Advanced Research Projects Agency Network (ARPANET) formed. Chris references the 1962 Douglas Engelbart article titled "Augmented Human intellect." This insightful article describes how our intellectual capacity would change by using technology to augment our own internal biological-based memory. Through technology with digital memory, which went beyond our human capacity, it would give us the ability to recall a vast database of memory at a moment's notice. The modern Internet achieves that success to a certain degree but Augmented Reality takes it to whole new levels. Chris' main point is the journey that ARPA took historically in forming the Internet can be compared to the ongoing journey of Augmented Reality. Although most people think AR is new, it is not but rather a type of technology that was unsupported by the existing capabilities of that time. The interface has been limited to the available technology. It is really only now that we are getting to the point where the miniaturization of hardware is reaching the point where we can start having implementations that are much closer to these original theories. If we look at the movie "Back to the Future" starring Michael J. Fox and Christopher Lloyd, the character Doc Brown (Lloyd) did not have access to Plutonium to power the "flux-capacitor", the heart of the time travel mechanism, in the year 1955. He needed to substitute the plutonium with a lightning bolt to generate the "1.21 gigawatts" of electricity to kick start the time machine and get Marty back to 1985. Modern-day bandwidth, microprocessors, miniature computing form factors, high-end video, location-based GPS, and a host of other factors are the "Plutonium" that AR needs to be successful. When it comes to the future of AR, Chris would not be surprised if a sort of AR transition device becomes available like the device DoCoMo's "AR Walker." The device clips on to a person's eye glasses and has a small monocular-type screen that goes in front of the person's eye. The device can show AR-type visuals as the person moves their head and looks around (Figure 5.2).

FIGURE 5.2 DoCoMo's AR Walker

He believes that these types of devices, similar to how the Bluetooth standard became popular, could become common because of the potential for high data rate transfers of video between your device in your pocket and the attached AR visual clip on display. He predicts we might see an array of products along that line coming on to the market in the next couple of years. These transition devices will lead to a more robust-type product that is actually built into the eyewear products. It is hard to speculate on the time frame but Chris hopes it is sooner than 6–8 years away. Chris believes when the true transition takes place—nobody will call it AR anymore. Particularly in the mobile space, an AR user interface is going to eventually become the standard user interface for mobile devices. It will become a ubiquitous mobile computing interface from that point on. This could be the roadmap for the next decade.

Helen Papagiannis

Another rising star in the AR art world is Helen Papagiannis. Helen is an artist, designer, PhD researcher, consultant, and international presenter on the topic of Augmented Reality. Helen has travelled around the world talking about the power of AR and the influence it can have on art. As people become exposed to AR for the first time, Helen has been bombarded with many questions on how AR works and what newcomers should expect from this unfamiliar concept. Helen has become the unofficial "AR Evangelist" spreading the good word on how Augmented Reality will shape the imaginative psyche. She sees an AR movement unfolding and her role, and passion, has become to champion, educate, and inspire the masses on how AR can be extended as a new visual medium. She sees the power that AR can have on the creative ability and artistic perspective of designers and storytellers to enhance the human condition. Helen defines Augmented Reality as "a layering of digital elements (such as text, audio, video, animations) atop reality where those elements are interactive and in real time."

Helen came from a design industry background and became introduced to the concept of AR in graduate studies in 2005. She had heard about Virtual Reality but developed inquisitiveness on the new topic of Augmented Reality and vigorously researched it. She immediately saw the potential for AR in design, in art, and in a new visual medium that was never seen before. The first AR demo she experienced had a profound impact on her and triggered the wonderment of how art, design, and storytelling could be expanded.

According to Helen, the overall best feature of AR is that it can make the invisible visible. This is why art can flourish in the world of AR. Helen is also excited about how AR can be intertwined with a sense of touch, or haptics. She says that up until now the only tactile element of AR has been our physical world and that which really exists in our physical environment. AR haptics has completely changed that because now we can touch and change the virtual and have instantaneous feedback.

Helen's role during a presentation at the 2011 *International Symposium on Mixed and Augmented Reality (ISMAR)* conference focused on the role of the artist and evolving AR as a new medium. One main goal of her presentation was to influence artists and storytellers, and other creative people to get more involved in AR. Many of these creative talents may not necessarily have a technical or programming background. By creating dialog between artists and the AR technical community, she hopes to push AR forward as a new medium and to challenge the artistic community to ask questions and collaborate to develop tools that artists and storytellers need that are critical to understand the specific capabilities and unique attributes of AR. Helen sees AR currently positioned in much the same way that motion pictures were 100 years ago.

Helen's artistic inspiration came from Georges Méliès who took his background of being a magician and helped transform early cinema and became a successful filmmaker. Georges brought his magic tricks and creativity to the stage of cinema. In Helen's eyes he was a real pioneer and innovator. He understood how magical cinema was developing and infused a real wonderment to the medium. Helen wants to leverage and harness those unique characteristics of other successful mediums to create something entirely new through Augmented Reality. She sees more artists and the artistic influence in the AR community growing, as more AR tools are available, so they can work directly with the medium. A great place to learn about Helen and her research is at her blog Augmented Stories:

http://arnews.tv/ARnewsTV.
http://www.arshowcase.com/.
http://www.scoop.it/t/augmented-reality-the-future-of-the-internet.

COMPANIES SPECIALIZING IN AR
Total Immersion

Total Immersion, founded in 1998 provides the most widely used commercial Augmented Reality platform. Powering over 1000 projects within the last 2 years with its proprietary patented platform, Total Immersion focuses on creating rich, immersive environments and gameplay blurring the line between the physical and digital worlds. Total Immersion is considered the market leader for AR software and production quickly becoming a worldwide phenomenon, serving a growing international client roster including major advertising agencies and Fortune 500 brands in industries ranging from automotive, e-commerce, media, entertainment, toys and eyewear to apparel, accessories, and food and beverages (see Figure 5.3):

www.t-immersion.com

Google X

Google X is Google's R&D lab currently they are working on an interactive heads-up display called Project Glass which has created an incredible amount of buzz in the world of Augmented Reality. Google has made significant strides throughout 2012 and plans to make Project Glass available in 2013. Project Glass

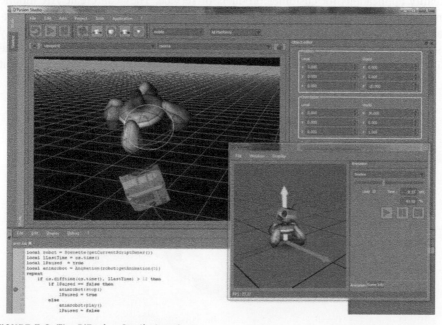

FIGURE 5.3 The D'Fusion Studio Interface

came about from trying to solve an interesting and challenging problem: trying to get technology out of the way while allowing people to still be connected out in the real world.

The technology is a wearable glasses-type form factor that covers the right eye (Figure 5.4). This gives the wearer a heads-up display view of the world while incorporating view sharing and social networking capabilities (Figure 5.5). Currently the input device is a considerable challenge because there is no physical keyboard. Google is experimenting with voice activation, gestures, and various types of touch interfaces. Google is also very concerned about societal acceptance and style. If these types of networked glasses are uncomfortable or embarrassing to wear then people simply won't use them.

Google has announced that they will be selling Project Glass devices for $1500 and will ship by early 2013.

Gravity Jack

Gravity Jack is a company that came together in 2009 and has assembled a self-proclaimed dream team of developers. Gravity Jack's CEO, Luke Richey who relays their mission "is to give Grandma a reason to use Augmented Reality." They have now teamed up with ARToolworks and are considered a leading technology provider when it comes to AR. Gravity Jack specializes in developing Augmented Reality applications for customer products or service. They can create AR mobile and social games and write custom AR applications for mobile, Mac, and PC platforms. Gravity Jack can create facial recognition apps or allow Augmented Reality overlays for their clients. Gravity Jack utilizes the SiREAL World AR Platform. The SiREAL platform features IPS (Indoor Positioning System) that creates a mesh that

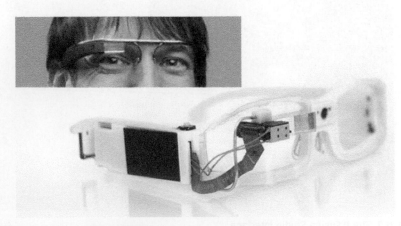

FIGURE 5.4 Google's Project Glass

FIGURE 5.5 The Wearer's View While Using Project Glass

allows the detection of the exact positioning of the device indoors. It's like utilizing an RFID tag indoor but knowing the exact coordinates of the device. SiREAL also uses Instant Mapping, Geolocation, Proximity Alert, and other features:

http://gravityjack.com

ARToolkit

Dr. Hirokazu Kato originally developed ARToolKit. The University of Washington Human Interface Technology Laboratory (HIT Lab), the University of Canterbury, (HIT Lab New Zealand), and Seattle's ARToolworks, Inc now supports it. It is a software library that is used to build AR applications. It uses square marker patterns, which are tracked by single camera position/orientation. ARtoolkit is free and distributed under the GNU (General Public License for Non-Commercial Uses).

Metaio

Metaio is a Germany-based company that has been doing some amazing work in the world of Augmented Reality. They now have a presence in San Franciso, CA. Metaio came on the scene in 1999 and began working on AR research. They are the developers of the Metaio technology platform and claim 10 million consumers that use their technology. Metaio considers their company to be a leader and pioneer in the AR technology field. Their vision is to easily integrate the virtual into the real world. Metaio showcases an entire software suite: Mobile SDK, PC SDK, Web SDK, Design, Creator, Engineer, and the Junaio browser plugin:

www.metaio.com

Metaio Creator

The Metaio Creator is a drag and drop Augmented Reality software product that allows someone to create a complete AR scenario in approximately 5 min. The tool is designed to allow the print and publishing industry to enhance their media with AR. The Metaio Creator uses a simple three-step workflow shown in Figure 5.6.

Junaio

Metaio created the Augmented Reality browser Junaio that was designed for custom mobile AR uses. It displays Junaio channels that can be utilized by third-party applications. Channels can utilize location-based Augmented Reality to show points of interest:

www.junaio.com

Layar

Layar is a another popular Augmented Reality company with roots in The Netherlands. The company history started in 2007 when three members came together to form

FIGURE 5.6 The Metaio Creator Interface

the trio that would launch SPRX Mobile in 2008. Vernor Vinge's novel Rainbows End inspired the company to explore content overlayed in reality. Layar created their Layar Reality Browser which has been installed over 10 million times which enhances real-world objects with digital information. Third-party developers can publish AR content on their open mobile platform:

www.layar.com

AR TOOLS

http://www.arsights.com/ ARsights.
http://studierstube.icg.tugraz.at/handheld_ar/artoolkitplus.php (ARtoolkit Plus).
http://artoolkit-tools.sourceforge.net/ (ARtoolkit).
http://www.artoolworks.com/community/osgart/ (OSGART).
http://sourceforge.net/projects/atomic-project/ ATOMIC.
http://ari.sourceforge.net/ Augmented Reality Interface.
http://ccv.nuigroup.com/ CCV Community Beta.
http://www.cc.gatech.edu/projects/dart/ DART.
http://graphics.cs.columbia.edu/projects/goblin/ GoblinXNA.
http://www.layar.com/player/ Layar Player SDK.
http://nyatla.jp/nyartoolkit/wiki/index.php?FrontPage.en NyARToolkit.
http://sourceforge.net/projects/opencv-ar/ OpenCV-AR.
http://sourceforge.net/projects/opencv-ar/ AR SDK.
http://sourceforge.net/projects/simpleaugmented/ SimpleAugmentedReality.
http://slartoolkit.codeplex.com/ SLARToolkit.
http://sourceforge.net/projects/sudara/ SudaRA.
http://touchless.codeplex.com/ Touchless SDK.

AR BLOGS

http://www.ardirt.com/ Augmented Reality Dirt Podcast & Blog.
http://augmentation.wordpress.com/ Augmentation.
http://augmentedblog.wordpress.com/ Augmented Blog.
http://www.augmented.org/blog/ Augmented.org.
http://www.augmentedlegality.com Augmented Legality Blog.
http://artimes.rouli.net/ Augmented Times.
http://gamesalfresco.com/ Games Alfresco.
http://www.kzero.co.uk/blog/category/augmented-reality/ Kzero Blog.
http://medicalaugmentedreality.com/ Medical Augmented Reality Blog.
http://augmentedrealityoverview.blogspot.com/ Augmented Reality Overview Blog.

SUMMARY

This chapter describes some of the groups, innovators, and resources that have pushed Augmented Reality in a positive direction. Each day we see new uses for Augmented Reality and the creation of new start-up companies that understand the groundbreaking potential that AR can have on society. Although Augmented Reality has been around for decades, its recent impact and growth is positioned to revolutionize technology like never before. Augmented Reality collaboration, meet-ups, and global sharing has created a community that is expanding and mainstreaming AR products. Smartphone and mobile platforms are creating new opportunities for apps and practical uses for the general public. This chapter highlights the impact of groups, organizations, and innovators that are rapidly changing the Augmented Reality and digital landscape.

Visions of the Future

INFORMATION IN THIS CHAPTER:

- The Big Trends
- Technical Trends
- Future Concepts for Augmented Reality
- AR Contact Lenses

INTRODUCTION

Up to this point we've looked at all the big aspects of present-day and emerging Augmented Reality. In this chapter we're going to take a couple of steps back and look at some of the larger global and social trends that are happening around us and how they will affect Augmented Reality (and many other things). We'll begin by exploring the economic and social trends that are taking place and then focus our attention on technical trends and some of the existing and emerging technologies that will directly support Augmented Reality and its continued adoption. Then we'll conclude this chapter by looking past the year 2020 into other technologies that, once developed for practical use, will push Augmented Reality to incredible new heights.

The Fifth K-Wave

K-waves, short for Kondratieff waves, are repeating techno-economic cycles that occur in the modern world economy. They were first noticed by the Russian economist Nikolai Kondratieff in 1925 and each wave averages between forty and sixty years in length. These waves have consistently followed the cycles where new technologies and industries develop while destroying the older obsolete ones that came before them.

Since the Industrial Revolution began in 1771 there have been five K-waves:

First Wave: 1771—The Industrial Revolution.
Second Wave: 1829—Steam Engine and Railways.
Third Wave: 1875—Steel and Heavy Engineering.

Fourth Wave: 1908—Petroleum, the Automobile, Mass Production.
Fifth Wave: 1971—Information Technology.

During the Fifth Wave there have been additional smaller waves that occur roughly every decade. Each decade in the Fifth Wave has created an enabling technology that has consistently pushed us forward. It began in 1970s when the microprocessor began being used by businesses. In the 1980s the personal computer was introduced forever changing the business landscape and bringing the computer into the home. In the 1990s the communications laser and optical media were the enabling technology allowing for networking and new types of telecommunications...the age of the Internet had arrived.

In the 2000s cheap sensors were widely distributed from RFID chips to mobile devices to the expanded use of the global positioning system (GPS).

In the 2010s it is likely that advanced automation will be the enabling technology. RedBox kiosks, self-checkout grocery lanes, automation systems in cars that aid drivers without their direct involvement, and so on. Additionally thanks to the build-up from the previous four decades there have emerged three forces that will continue to carry our technology development forward. The first is cheap computing devices which is everything from a PC to a mobile phone to a car's computer system. The second is ever increasing and the available bandwidth which is connecting everyone and everything to everyone and everything else. And third is the continued growth of open standards which allow for more and more systems to link with one another.

With all this momentum the new reality is there are really very few limiting factors to continued progress. With the technology available today the advances are so rapid that they have outpaced the applications that can take advantage of them. Ideal conditions for the continued improvement and development of Augmented Reality and many other disruptive technologies.

THE BIG TRENDS

In this section we'll cover several large trends that are not only shaping technology, but society. These trends will have considerable impact on what technology we choose to use as well as how we live and work in the future. We'll look at the new generation that is emerging, the changes taking place in Universities, and the video games that are being repurposed as learning tools.

Generation C: The Connected Generation

As we have shown, and most people are readily aware of, technology continues to integrate into our lifestyles at an ever-accelerating rate. These tools have transformed the way we communicate and use information both for work and for personal use. While we have embraced these technologies in the developed world, beginning with the telephone, they for the most part have served us by overlaying on our existing habits and lifestyles.

Today a new generation is emerging that has never experienced a world without the Internet, mobile devices, and social networking and they are fundamentally different from previous generations. This generation was born after 1990 and has lived their adolescent years after 2000 have been labeled "The Connected Generation" or Generation C because they are continuously connecting, communicating, social networking, searching, and clicking. They all have mobile phones but tend to prefer sending text messages rather than talking with people on the phone. Many of their social interactions take place on the Internet where they feel free to express their opinions and attitudes.

By the year 2020 they will make up 40% of the population in the United States, Europe, and the BRIC (Brazil, Russia, India, and China) countries, and 10% of the rest of the world. They will also constitute the largest single group of consumers worldwide. This combination of consumer buying power and their familiarity with technology along with their desire to remain in contact with large networks of family members, friends, business contacts, and people with common interests will transform how society will work and consume.

As Generation C comes into its own during this decade business traditions from the 20th Century will also begin to fade. Today 77 million Boomers are beginning to reach the traditional retirement age. Generation X has been in the workforce for a couple of decades and the next group, called Generation Y, is entering the workforce. Generation Y likes to engage in multi-tasking, they get bored easily, and they enjoy change. Generation Y and Generation C have a great deal in common and this will have a wide range of effects on how members of Generation C use communications technology, how they access and consume information and entertainment, and how they interact. These effects will be determined in part by the progress and development of technologies over the course of the next decade.

With this fundamental change occurring within an entire generation it raises and interesting question: "What will this do for the development of AR?" This generation wasn't around in the 1990s when VR attempted its rise and failed. The culture wasn't right, along with the technological infrastructure, but that would have been secondary had the people using the technology embraced it to the degree that Generation C is embracing today's technology. While the preceding generations also share these technologies with them, the connected generation has a common "connected mindset" that sets them apart in ways that will be unique in human history. It's this uniqueness that will foster the development of existing technologies in new and unseen ways.

The Evolving University

As business, education, and technology continue to intersect, a new trend has emerged that will disrupt the conventional 19th Century education model. This trend is how the Web is being used for education. In a 12-year study by the US Department of Education they concluded that people learn more effectively online than in traditional classrooms. This is due to the change that online students are familiar and comfortable with an online environment and that they are not faced with an authority figure. Today many Universities offer online distance learning degree programs which has changed the educational experience by allowing it to be infinitely customized. This change completely disrupts the traditional one-size-fits-all curriculum model. This new educational model is also able to make relevant suggestions for further learning, greatly increasing the speed and efficiency of learning. Additionally these types of adaptive, web-based systems will quickly migrate to mobile devices and from there be adapted into an Augmented Reality environment.

Changing Education and Training

With this changing trend in education other factors will also contribute to the evolution of education and training. These tools and approaches which have been pioneered by universities and corporations are starting to work their way down to primary and secondary education. Clayton Christensen highlights in his book, Disrupting Class, that these new technologies offer the potential to disrupt the prevailing 19th century educational paradigm with the shift starting in the results-oriented world of corporate training, and work its way down to the bureaucracy of K-12 public education.

This year, in 2012, video game style training programs are beginning to revolutionize vocational training as well as the development of other life skills. As discussed in Chapter 3, the AR movie "The Witness" has the potential to be repurposed to teach someone not just a vocational process but also how to interact with different types of people and situations at the same time. Another, and more familiar example is airline pilots who have for decades used flight simulators to practice the skills they need to fly a real jet. This subject will be explored further in the next section: Video Games—A Learning Tool.

According to a recent study highlighted in Strategy + Business, despite layoffs and corporate restructuring, savvy executives are seeing education as the opportunity of the future for at least five reasons:

1. Education improves productivity.
2. Companies can gain a competitive advantage by making their employees more competent and giving them broader "skill sets."
3. Learning improves morale, because workers realize that the company is not only planning on being around, but it is planning on keeping its employees around, too.
4. The shift to a knowledge economy. The 19th century model of a corporation, employees were trained in a rote task and then simply repeated it until they retired. Today, employees have to be able to think critically and analytically, to solve problems, and to innovate.
5. The aging of the Baby Boomers.

Successful companies that use this new educational paradigm will appeal to younger employees who are used to interacting online. Along with online learning and gamine, peer-to-peer learning is also part of this trend. Peer-to-peer learning allows for mass customization of the material which gives workers an opportunity to share what they know with others. This also allows employees to access the learning materials on their own schedule, making learning less disruptive to normal business operations. As this trend continues Augmented Reality will complement this new training and education model.

Video Games: A Learning Tool

Today, as much as it might surprise some people, new research indicates that video games are not only not a waste of time, but they are actually a powerful tool for learning, that just might separate tomorrow's most skilled, productive, and successful performers from the rest of their generation.

Consider a few statistics that show how widespread the use of video games is for today's American youth:

* By age 6, 30% of all children have played a video game.
* The average 8–12 year-old plays video games 13 h per week.
* The average 13–18-year-old plays video games 14 h per week.
* The average college freshman has spent 10,000 h playing video games, compared to just 5000 h reading.
* More than 80% of 8–19-year-olds have at least one game console at home.
* In the US, sales of video and computer games, as well as game consoles, exceeded $10 billion in 2006.

It's commonly known that computer games are popular, but what makes them a positive force for teaching children and teenagers the skills they will need to excel in the workplace? Simply put, video game players must process multiple streams of information, just as the mind does in the real world. Cognitive scientists are finding that video game play actually helps develop important mental skills, such as concentration, systems thinking, and patience. The Federation of American Scientists has come out in favor of video games as a way to teach advanced mental skills, such as strategic thinking, problem solving, adapting to rapid change, forming and executing plans, and analyzing information.

These new findings indicate there is considerable potential for Augmented Reality gaming for both entertainment and education. Video games are designed in such a way so that they actually exploit one of the key principles of learning, called the "regime of competence." This means that the game becomes increasingly more challenging as the player completes easier levels and gains competence. This creates a certain balance where the player doesn't get so good at the game that boredom sets in nor is game so frustrating that the player gives up. With this new trend taking hold, in time video gamers will bring an extraordinary set of skills to the corporate world. As authors John C. Beck and Mitchell Wade explain in *The Kids Are Alright: How the Gamer Generation is Changing the Workplace*.

These new skills include the following:

- They have developed an unprecedented ability to multi-task.
- They place a high value on being an expert.
- They creatively solve problems.
- They calculate risks and know the importance of getting a good return on investments.
- They are not afraid of competition.
- They love to win.

Today new workers will also place much more emphasis on being happy in their jobs. Workers will also be looking for an atmosphere of collaborative decision making particularly if they grew up playing multiplayer games. It is highly likely that the companies that provide this type of work environment will be able to build and retain a much more productive workforce.

TECHNICAL TRENDS

Along with societal changes there continue to be significant technical trends that shape our world while quietly propelling Augmented Reality ever forward. Some of these technical trends include the Internet of Things, the expanding video game market as well as a variety of support technologies that will improve and enhance Augmented Reality systems and the overall experience.

The Internet of Things

The Internet of Things, or IoT, refers to a world where sensors and actuators are embedded into physical objects and are linked through the wireless and wired networks that all live and interact with one another. These networks will often use the same Internet Protocol (IP) that is the standard for the Internet. The Internet of Things is altering the physical world in such a way that objects, whether physical or virtual, can be searched, tracked, and interacted with seamlessly making the world as a whole a type of information system.

The Internet of Things will have wide-ranging influences in the areas of information analysis and Automation and Control. The Internet of Things will be useful for information and analysis functions by:

1. Tracking behavior.
2. Creating enhanced situational awareness.
3. Providing sensor-driven analytics.

The Internet of Things will be useful for Automation and Control functions by allowing for:

1. Process optimization.
2. Optimized resource consumption.
3. Complex autonomous systems.

From this list of functions Augmented Reality will play the largest role in further enabling situational awareness. Data from large numbers of sensors, deployed in the existing infrastructure such as roads and buildings, can give decision makers a heightened awareness of real-time events, particularly when the sensors are combined with advanced display or Augmented Reality technologies. For example, security personnel would be able to utilize a combination of video, audio and in some cases vibration sensors to detect people who enter an area without authorization. These sensors can also be used to report on environmental conditions such as weather and ocean currents; the potential is limited only by the need. As the Internet of Things and Augmented Reality continue to develop, it is probable that AR will become one of the predominate interfaces for the IoT in much the same way that the graphical user interface (GUI) became the interface for the Internet.

The Expanding Video Game Market

According to PricewaterhouseCoopers, in 2006 they estimated that the video game software market was $31.1 billion worldwide. Compare this to box office revenues from movie theaters which were $33.6 billion in 2006 and the size and popularity of the video game market becomes clear. In the past most technological advances have been driven, either directly or indirectly, by the needs of the military. But that is changing. Today many of the major technological advances are made in the commercial marketplace. The reason for this change is the commercial marketplace which has two distinct advantages over the military. They are volume and capital. Demand for a product creates the volume which brings down cost and makes items affordable, which in turn creates more demand. And capital, specifically the freedom to use it, gives businesses the ability to take risks with assets on unproven ideas, while politicians (theoretically) have to think twice about risking taxpayer money.

Present day games have animations and special effects that rival some big-budget movies and contain compelling characters, life-like landscapes and a strong plot. These new games also set themselves apart from movies because they are interactive rather than passive allowing the player to control the action and influence the story rather than just sitting back and watching.

"Exergames" and AR

An "exergame" is defined as an entertaining video game that combines game play with exercise (Figure 6.1). Researchers found that the use of exergames significantly improved the mood and mental health of older adults with depression. A Society for Neuroscience report concluded that repeated exercise, even in a virtual environment, helped stroke patients improve arm and hand function. Augmented Reality could be used to create a rich exergame user experience by allowing the real world to be the place for exercise while the augmentation provides the entertainment. In time, perhaps the stereotype of the lethargic, couch potato gamer will be replaced by that of an eco-challenge contestant who rather than having to cross virtual terrain in World of Warcraft or Halo will have to cross real terrain instead.

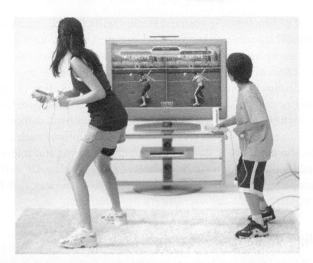

FIGURE 6.1 An Exergame on the Nintendo Wii

Augmented Reality Enhancers

Augmented Reality is a suite of capabilities that relies on many different technologies to function properly. Along with the growth of the Internet of Things and gaming technologies as well as the social and demographic shifts, this next section will quickly highlight some other technologies that are being developed which will directly benefit Augmented Reality and its widespread adoption:

- *Gesture-based remote control:* A camera in your PC, TV, or DVD player will automatically pick up and interpret your gestures and use them as commands. We're seeing this today with the Kinect.
- *Universal wireless standards:* With the continued global adoption of mobile phones eventually all phones will operate anywhere, anytime. When these universal wireless standards become the norm, Augmented Reality systems will leverage these new standards.
- *Avatars:* According to Forbes, virtual worlds populated by avatars will be a big part of business in the future. Parks Associates, a firm specializing in virtual worlds, estimates that there will be 33 million adults with avatars in virtual worlds by 2013. With this growing trend it will be commonplace to see avatars regularly intermingled with a real crowd as AR technology becomes commonplace.
- *Machine vision:* This will become more available and more sophisticated over the next 5–15 years. Machines that can see will have capabilities far beyond that of people being able to see not only the visible light bands but infrared, ultraviolet, and multispectral. Augmented Reality markers that are based on visual cues will be far more customizable and robust when they can be identified by more than one band of the spectrum.

- *Cloud computing:* Cloud computing is a service by which a company can store information and get software service from a remote provider. Cloud computing will expand to accommodate the Connected Generation's desire to access their 24/7 virtual life from a variety of devices. With cloud computing, their information and applications will not need to reside on distinct devices, but rather will be available anytime, anywhere, through any device, via the Cloud.

As more and more supporting technologies continue to develop and work their way into the consumer space the potential for rich AR environments and real-time interaction will appear first in games and then be leveraged by businesses as workers become more dispersed globally. In time these AR experiences will be so robust that team members in adjoining cubicles will choose to meet in these object-rich environments.

FUTURE CONCEPTS FOR AUGMENTED REALITY

So far we've discussed the potential for Augmented Reality by focusing on existing technologies and current trends but now let's move forward to a few decades into the future. As the Fifth Wave becomes part of history and the Sixth Wave emerges, bringing with it the "GNR Revolution", which stands for Genetics, Nanotechnology, and Robotics we will have whole new potentials for developing and using Augmented Reality.

AR CONTACT LENSES

The most functional form-factor for Augmented Reality would be in the form of contact lenses. This is the approach that Babak Parviz, a bionanotechnology expert at the University of Washington, in Seattle, is working to create. Parviz has built a lens with one embedded LED, which is powered wirelessly. It's a step forward but barely hints at what will soon be possible with this technology. Today conventional contact lenses are polymers formed in specific shapes to correct poor vision. Parviz intends to take this type of lens and turn into a functional Augmented Reality system with integrated control, communication, and antenna circuits (Figure 6.2). These components will eventually include hundreds of LEDs, which will form images in front of the eye, such as words, charts, and photographs. A separate, portable device will relay displayable information to the lens's control circuit, which will operate the electronics embedded in the lens. The good news is these lenses don't have to be terribly complex to be useful. Basic image processing combined with Internet access would allow a contact lens of this type to view whole new worlds of visual information without the constraints of a physical display.

However, there are three fundamental challenges standing in the way of building this type of multipurpose contact lens. The first is the manufacturing process. Many of the lens's parts and subsystems are incompatible with one another and with the

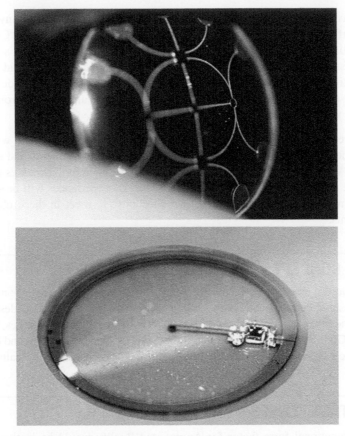

FIGURE 6.2 A Prototype AR Contact Lens

fragile polymer of the lens. This in turn leads to the second challenge in which all the components of the lens need to be miniaturized and integrated into a small, flexible, transparent polymer. And the third challenge is that the lens needs to be completely safe for the eye.

Fortunately, in spite of these challenges, all the basic technologies needed to build functional Augmented Reality contact lenses are in place. Parviz feels the true promise of his research isn't just the actual system he thinks of making, but whether it is a display or a sensor or both. He sees a future where the once humble contact lens becomes a real development platform, much like the iPhone is today, with thousands of developers contributing their ideas and inventions.

Biomimicry and Bionic Eyes

The word "bionics" comes from the combination of the words biology and electronics and is the study of mechanical systems that function like living organisms or parts of living organisms. As we move into the Sixth Wave and nanotechnology advances, the implications for medical treatment as well as physical enhancement are profound. While still very much in its infancy the idea of bionic eyes is no longer science fiction. Mark Humayun, an ophthalmologist at the University of Southern California and a company called Second Sight, has recently helped a woman named Jo Ann Lewis regain her vision.

Jo Ann Lewis lost her sight years ago to retinitis pigmentosa, a degenerative disease that destroys light-detecting cells in the eyes called rods and cones. Between 1992 and 2006 Humayun, with the aid of his patients, began to understand the language the inner retina spoke or how to feed it images it could understand and after a decade of testing Humayun and his colleagues developed a system they dubbed Argus.

Using the Argus system, patients wore a pair of dark glasses with a tiny video camera mounted on them, along with a radio transmitter. Video signals were beamed to a computer worn on a belt, translated to electrical impulse patterns understood by ganglion cells, and then beamed to a receiver resting behind the ear. From there a wire took them inside the eye, to a square array of 16 electrodes gently attached to the retinal surface. The impulses triggered the electrodes. The electrodes triggered the cells. Then the brain did the rest, enabling these first patients to see edges and some coarse shapes.

In the fall of 2006 Humayun, Second Sight, and an international team increased the electrodes in the array to 60. Like a camera with more pixels, the new array produced a sharper image. Lewis, from Rockwall, Texas, was among the first to get one (Figure 6.3). "Now I'm able to see silhouettes of trees again," she says. "That's one of the last things I remember seeing naturally. Today I can see limbs sticking out this way and that."

FIGURE 6.3 Jo Ann Lewis Using the ARGUS system

Now this type of technology is possible, and over time more and more practical, it's not difficult to imagine Augmented Reality being blended in with bionic vision of the future giving those who need it the ability to see the real and digital world at the same time.

Nanotechnology

Nanotechnology is the engineering of materials at an incredibly tiny scale; a nanometer, or a billionth of a meter. For comparison, a human hair is about 80,000 nanometers wide. Nanoscale materials are often less than 100 nanometers in size. This new field is expected to be the next industrial revolution and has the potential to transform everything from supercomputers to medicine.

Surgery is considered one of the greater advances in medical history but is still and invasive and traumatic process. With the continuing advances in nanotechnology, a whole new generation of robots is coming. At the Technion-Israel Institute of Technology they have designed a robot that can crawl through the bloodstream to treat conditions, such as tumors, that are too difficult for conventional surgery. The robot is called ViRob and is only 1 millimeter in diameter (Figure 6.4). ViRob is powered by an external magnetic field and has the ability to crawl upstream against the flow of blood. The researchers say that numerous ViRob robots could be injected into the body and remain there indefinitely carrying out medical procedures as needed.

American researchers are working on a medical micro-robot called HeartLander which is designed to provide therapy to the surface of a beating heart (Figure 6.5).

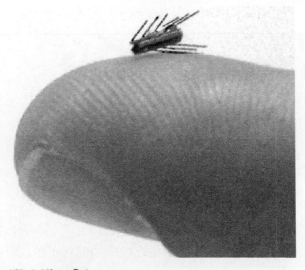

FIGURE 6.4 The ViRob Micro-Bot

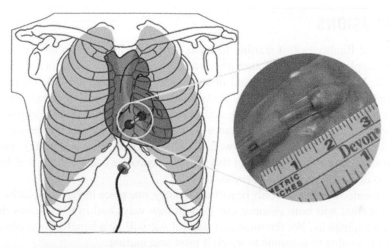

FIGURE 6.5 The HeartLander Micro-Bot

This micro-bot is inserted through a small incision and attaches itself to the surface of the heart where it can then inject drugs or be used to install other medical devices to help control ailments such as congestive heart failure.

Scientists at the Swiss Federal Institute of Technology in Zurich have developed a nanoscale propulsion system that mimics the flagella that propel some bacteria. This system is just 27 nanometers thick and 40 micrometers long which means they will be able to create medical micro-bots far smaller than anything seen before. Bots of this size will be capable of going into the tiniest blood vessels and even inside cancerous tumors.

Bionics, Nanotechnology, and Augmented Reality

With the previous sections in mind, it is almost inevitable that bionic vision and nanotechnology will intersect as soon as technically possible. In fact, the Augmented Reality technology of today may aid in the development of future nanotechnology by allowing engineers to us AR as the interface for the design of nano-sized robots and creating an interesting symbiosis. In the future Augmented Reality may be credited as one of the enablers for the very nanotechnology that will be attached directly to a person's eye allowing projecting Augmented Reality directly onto their retinas. This concept was illustrated in the science fiction best-seller "Pandora's Star" by Peter F. Hamilton where the people in the story used "virtual vision", an Augmented Reality interface that blended seamlessly with a person's natural vision. With this imagined ideal, and the continued pace of technological advancement, it is possible that this option will be available to Generation C by the time they reach middle age.

CONCLUSIONS

Augmented Reality is just starting to break out of its infancy, because of this the possible applications in the future are tremendous. As we've described throughout the book AR is already being used in some very interesting and innovative ways. Moving beyond what is technically possible we do see social acceptance issues and privacy concerns arising, and being addressed, as Augmented Reality applications become more robust. Social acceptance will stem from the need for devices to be subtle, discrete, and unobtrusive as well as fashionably acceptable. Privacy concerns will arise in a variety of ways, but this will be true of any technology that has the ability to detect and recognize people.

Augmented Reality will only be part of the story; one piece in the larger technology landscape, that will both enhance our lives in new ways and in some cases disturb and even frighten us. For the most part we feel AR will be a benefit to people and it will be interesting to continue to watch it grow and mature.

Glossary

A

ARDesktop: A three-dimensional desktop interface with controls and widgets utilizing an ARToolKit class library.

Alternate Reality Game (ARG): interactive narrative that utilizes the real world as a platform. It usually involves game elements and multiple media to relay a story that may be affected by a participants actions or ideas.

Augmented Reality: the combining of real and virtual information that is interactive in real time and is rendered in 3D.

Augmented ID: a tool similar to Recognizr that uses facial recognition to identify the person and associate them with personal information or social networks.

AR-Quake: an Augmented Reality extension to the popular desktop game Quake.

Archeoguide: a mobile AR system for cultural heritage sites.

AR Browser: a method of using Augmented Reality where the application brings the web into the world around you.

ARTag: Non-commercial license that is an alternative to ARTookit that utilizes complex image processing and substitute to ARToolkit.

ARToolkit: computer vision tracking library developed for the creation of AR applications that overlay virtual imagery on the real world.

ATOMIC Authoring Tool: Front end for the ARToolkit library developed for non-programmers to create simple and small Augmented Reality applications, released under the GNU GPL License. It is a Cross-platform Authoring Tool software.

ARToolkitPlus: targeted for handheld users and developers that extends the usage of ARToolkit. This is no longer developed.

Affective computing: aims to make computers more aware of the emotional state of their users and able to adapt accordingly.

Annotation and visualization: This is what most mobile browsers do. Tell you about what you're looking at, where things are.

143

Augmented Virtuality: refers to the merging of real world objects into virtual worlds. It is also referred to as Mixed reality.

B

Battlefield Augmented Reality System (BARS): The system consists of a wearable computer, a wireless network system and a see-through HMD. The system targets the augmentation of a battlefield scene.

C

Camera re-sectioning: the process of finding the true parameters of the camera that produced a given photograph or video.

Cave Automatic Virtual Environment (CAVE): an immersive virtual reality environment where projectors are directed to three, four, five, or six of the walls of a room-sized cube.

Compositing: the combination of visual elements from separate sources into single images, often to create the illusion that all those elements are parts of the same scene.

Closed-view HMD: A head-mounted display that does not allow any direct view of the real world.

CyberCodes: a visual tagging system designed for augmented reality (AR) applications, based on an image recognition technology that uses visual-markers.

D

Distributed Cognition: the ability to interact meaningfully with tools that expand mental capacities.

DART: The Designers Augmented Reality Toolkit: a set of software tools for Macromedia Director that support the design and implementation of augmented reality experiences and applications.

Dynamic errors: are the ones that have no effect until either the viewpoint or the objects begin moving.

E

End-to-End System Delay: defined as the time difference between the moment that the tracking system measures the position and orientation of the viewpoint to the moment when the generated images corresponding to that position and orientation appear in the displays.

F

FPV: First Person View: a graphical perspective rendered from the viewpoint of the person.

Fiducials: fixed points reference points or lines within a scene to which other objects can be related or against which objects can be measured.

G

Geo-tagging: a process of adding geographical identification metadata to various media. Geo-tagging can help users find a wide variety of location-specific information.

H

HMD/HWD & HUD • HMD: Terms Helmet-Mounted and Head- Mounted are used interchangeably and there is a movement to introduce instead a very general term. HMD places images of both the physical world and registered virtual graphical objects over the user's view of the world.

Head-Up Displays (HUDs): any transparent display that presents data without requiring the user to look away from his or her usual viewpoint.

Haptics: the sense of touch.

Hybrid user interfaces: the use of different display and input technologies and reap the benefits of each technology for the purposes for which it is best suited.

Human Machine Interface: typically computerized in complex systems. It utilizes tools for incorporating the human factors in the interface design are developed based on knowledge of computer science, such as operating systems programming languages and human graphics.

I

Image-based modeling and rendering (IBMR): method that relies on a set of two-dimensional images of a scene to generate a three-dimensional model and then render some novel views of this scene.

Intelligence Amplification (IA): using the computer as a tool to make a task easier for a human to perform.

Internet of Things: the combination of searchable, identifiable objects and their virtual representations in an Internet-like structure.

L

Local Feature Extraction: tries to identify salient parts of the object within the image. The system also tracks the object's movement, and works out its orientation. This is necessary in order to know how the virtual data should be positioned in relation to the object.

LLE marker: an Augmented Reality marker based on latitude, longitude and elevation.

M

Milgram's Reality: Virtuality Continuum (1994) Paul Milgram and Fumio defined a continuum that spans form the real environment to a pure virtual environment. Augmented Reality and Augmented Virtuality fall in between the real environment and the pure virtual environment.

Mixed reality (MR): refers to the merging of real and virtual worlds to produce new environments and visualizations where physical and digital objects co-exist and interact in real time. A mix of reality, augmented reality, augmented virtuality and virtual reality.

Motion capture: applications track an actor's body parts to control a computer-animated character or for the analysis of an actor's movements. This is fine for position recovery, but not for orientation.

Mobile AR browser: see AR browser.

Marker: a digital marker or pattern that can be identified and tracked to allow an Augmented Reality experience.

Marker-less AR: software that is able to recognize natural features of an environment which creates more natural interactions between digital and physical world elements.

Massively Multiplayer Online Game (MMO): a multiplayer video game which is capable of supporting hundreds of players simultaneously.

N

NyARToolkit: Released for virtual machines under an ARToolkit class library for those which host Java, C#, and Android.

O

Optical see-through HMD: a head-mounted display that operates by placing optical combiners in front of the user's eyes.

Optical sensor: A device that measures a physical quantity and converts it into a signal which can be read by an observer or by an instrument.

OSGART: ARToolkit combined with OpenSceneGraph.

P

"Perfect Registration": the flawless alignment of real and virtual objects.

Pinhole Model: all the graphic objects, regardless of distance, are in focus.

Popcode: a new Markerless Augmented Reality (AR) platform which allows objects in the real world to be brought to life with interactive 3D content.

Parrot AR Drone: A remote-controlled device that flies utilizing a number of sensors, including a front camera, a vertical camera and an ultrasound altimeter. The AR parrot can be controlled by an iPhone, Android or similar controller.

Promethean Board: an interactive board that it used in a classroom environment that allows students to creatively participate in advanced learning techniques.

Q

Quick Response (QR) Codes: A QR code is a matrix barcode (or two-dimensional code), readable by QR scanner mobile phones with a smartphone or camera.

Quartz Composer: a node-based visual programming language provided as part of the Xcode development environment in Mac OS X for processing and rendering graphical data.

R

Real-time computer graphics: the subfield of computer graphics focused on producing and analyzing images in real time.

S

SLARToolkit – A Silverlight port of NyARToolkit

Spatial Augmented Reality (SAR): makes use of digital projectors to display graphical information onto physical objects. The key difference in SAR is that the display is separated from the users of the system. Spatial AR is a good candidate for collaborative work, as the users can see each others faces.

See-through HMD: lets the user see the real world, with virtual objects superimposed by optical or video technologies. HMD must be tracked with a six degree of freedom sensor. This tracking allows for the computing system to register the virtual information to the physical world.

Simulated reality: the proposition that reality could be simulated perhaps by computer simulation to a degree indistinguishable from "true" reality.

Static errors are the ones that cause registration errors even when the user's viewpoint and the objects in the environment remain completely still.

Social Proximity: a cumulative trust between two or more members within a geographical region that typically develops through user generated services or social applications.

Second Life: a virtual world operated by Linden Labs of San Francisco, CA, that has its own virtual economy and self-contained digital world.

T

Template matching: Template images of the real object are taken from a variety of viewpoints. These are used to search the digitized image for the real object. Once that is found, a virtual wireframe can be superimposed on the real object.

Touring Machine : the first mobile augmented reality system.

Trans-media Navigation: ability to follow the flow of information across multiple modalities.

V

Video tracking: the process of locating a moving object (or several ones) in time using a camera.

Visual-kinesthetic: the visual sense of body movement.

Visual-proprioceptive: the visual sense of the relative position of neighboring parts of the body and strength of effort being employed in movement.

Visual capture: the tendency of the brain to believe what it sees rather than what it feels, hears, etc.

Virtuality Continuum: a phrase used to describe a concept that there is a continuous scale ranging between the completely virtual, a Virtual Reality, and the completely real: Reality.

Virtual Environments (VE): a computer simulated environment.

Virtual retinal display (VRD), also known as a retinal scan display (RSD) or retinal projector: a display technology that draws a raster diplay (like a television) directly onto the retina of the eye.

Visualization: a mental image that is similar to visual perception.

Virtual Box Simulator: U.S. Postal Service augmented reality program that helps customers determine if objects will fit in shipping boxes.

Video Spatial Displays: visual displays, usually associated with gaming consoles that effect visual sensory perception.

Virtual Reality: a term that applies to computer-simulated environments that can simulate physical presence in places in the real world, as well as in imaginary worlds.

W

Wearable Displays: a display device, usually worn on the head or part of a helmet (see Head Mounted Display).

0–10

6DOF: six degrees of freedom – refers to the freedom of movement of a rigid body in three-dimensional space.

References

Aguilera, P. (2009, August 18). Digital info on the real world. MIT Technology Review.

Arnall, T. (2008, October 24). The web in the world fabric rblg.

Aron, J. (2012, January 31). AR goggles make crime scene investigation a desk job. New Scientist.

Augmented reality business conference (2010, April 23). 1st European AT Business Conference. Berlin.

Augmented Reality Flash Mob. <www.sndrv.nl/ARflashmob>.

Augmented reality glasses are at least 20 years away. <www.augmentedplanet.com>. August 18, 2010.

Azuma, R. (1996). A survey of augmented reality. Hughes Research Laboratories.

Azuma, R. Registration errors in augmented reality. <www.cs.unc.edu/~azuma/azuma_AR.html>.

Baker, S. (2005, February 14). The business of nanotech BusinessWeek.

Becker, G. (2010, May). Challenge, drama and social engagement: Designing mobile augmented reality experiences lighting laboratories.

Becker, G. (2010, June). Beyond augmented reality: Ubiquitous media experiences lighting laboratories.

Benjamin Gotow, J., Krzysztof Zienkiewicz, Jules White, & Douglas C. Schmidt (2011, February). Addressing challenges with augmented reality applications on smartphones. Vanderbilt University.

Bichlmeier, C., et al. Contextual anatomic mimesis. Hybrid in-situ visualization method for improving multi-sensory depth perception in medical augmented reality.

BMW group developing augmented reality windshield displays. MotoringFile. October 12, 2011.

Boulton, C. (2011, March 20). Meet google goggles, augmented reality vector. <Eweek.com>.

Buckner, G. (2011, May 2). College tuition reality check. FoxBusiness.

Callari, R. (2010, May 31). Facebook could face more privacy backlash with augmented reality QR codes. <Inventorspot.com>.

Callari, R. (2010, July 24). QR codes augmenting our lives from Tokyo to Manhattan. <Inventorspot.com>.

Callari, R. (2010, May 4). Hotels.com First to use augmented reality for virtual travel experience. <Inventorspot.com>.

Callari, R. (2010, June 12). Augmented reality sunglasses can insert social networking into your sights. <Inventorspot.com>.

Callari, R. (2010, May 13). Tagwhat, you're it! augmented reality is future of location-based social networks Inventorspot.com.

Callari, R. (2012, June 12). Could tag technology replace Google search? Inventorspot.com.

Callari, R. (xxxx). Augmented reality provides terminator eyesight InventorSpot.com. <http://inventorspot.com/articles/augmented_reality_provides_terminator_eyesight_32315>.

Cameron, C. (2010, June 11). Military-grade augmented reality could redefine modern warfare. New York Times.

Cass, S. (2011, January 7). CES: Face recognition on the fly MIT Technology Review.

Chen, B. (2009, August). If you're not seeing data, you're not seeing. Wired Magazine.

Christiansen, C., & Horn, M. (2008). Disrupting class: How disruptive innovation will change the way the World Learns. McGraw Hill.

Claburn, T. (2011, December 2). Gartner's 2012 Forecast: Cloudy, with widespread consumerization. InformationWeek.

CNN hologram technology may change web conferencing forever (2008, May 11). <www.labnol.org/internet/video/cnn-hologram-technology-for-web-conferencing/5219/>.

Coelho, E. M., MacIntyre, B. (2003, October 7). High-level tracker abstractions for augmented reality system design. International Workshop on Software Technology for AR Systems 2003 (STARS 2003). Tokyo, Japan.

Computer aided medical procedures & augmented reality (CAMP), Technische Universität München.

Curtis, S. (2009, October 26). Augmented reality's time is coming thanks to smarter smartphones. <Silicon.com>.

Delio, M. (2005, February 15). Augmented reality: Another (virtual) brick in the wall. MIT Technology Review.

Dubois, E., Laurence Nigay, J., Troccaz, O., Chavanon, & Carrat, L. (1999). Classification space for augmented surgery, an augmented reality case study. In Sasse, A., & Johnson, C. (Eds.), Proceedings of Interact'99 (pp. 353–359). Edinburgh (UK): IOS Press, June 2004.

Educause Learning Initiative (2005, September). 7 things you should know about Augmented Reality, Educause.

Feiner, S., Macintyre, B., & Seligmann, D. (1993). Knowledge-based augmented reality. *Commun. ACM* 36(7), 53–62.

Feiner, S. (2002, April 24). Augmented reality: A new way of seeing. Scientific American.

Fingas, J. (2012, July 3). Fujitsu, NICT create indoor navigation for the blind using ultrawideband, Android phones, kind hearts Fujitsu.

Gibson, J. (1966). The senses considered as perceptual systems. Boston: Houghton Mifflin.

Graham-Rowe, D. (2009, April 6). The best computer interfaces: Past, present, and future. MIT Technology Review.

Gray, J. (2011). Parrot AR Drone. Robot Magazine, January/February, 70–73.

Greene, K. (2009, February 24). Microsoft demos augmented vision. MIT Technology Review.

Greene, K. (2009, June 5). The display that watches you. MIT Technology Review.

Greene, J. (2012, July 2). My life as a cyborg. CNET News.

Grifantini, K. (October 26, 2009). Faster maintenance with augmented reality. MIT Technology Review.

Grifantini, K. (2010, December 28). The year in enhancing reality. MIT Technology Review.

Grifantini, K. (2010, January 29). Malleable maps, artistic robots and bubble interfaces. MIT Technology Review.

Grifantini, K. (2010, March 17). GM develops augmented reality windshield. MIT Technology Review.

Grifantini, K. (2010, February 11). Microsoft adds augmented reality to bing maps. MIT Technology Review.

Hamilton, J. (2009, October 20). Bionic eye opens new world of sight for blind. NPR.

Henderson, S. & Feiner, S. (2007, July). Augmented reality for maintenance and repair (armar). Technical Report AFRL-RH-WP-TR-2007-0112, United States Air Force Research Lab.

Henderson, S. J. & Feiner, S. (2009). Evaluating the benefits of augmented reality for task localization in maintenance of an armored personnel carrier turret. Mixed and augmented reality, IEEE/ACM International Symposium on, pp. 135–144.

Hidden Creative, Inc. (2011, March 22). Augmented reality marketing strategies: The how to guide for marketers.

Holden, W. (2011, February). A new reality for mobile. Juniper Research Limited.

iARM. <http://spill.tanagram.com/tag/iARM/>.

Jacob, R. J., Girouard, A., Hirshfield, L. M., & Horn, M. S. (2008). Reality-based interaction: A framework for post-WIMP interfaces (pp. 201–210). Florence, Italy: ACM Press, April 5–10.

James, W. (1907). Pragmatism: a new name for some old ways of thinking. New York: Longman Green and Co.

Jongedijk, L. A brief history of augmented reality (AR) and names of key researchers associated with AR. <http://augreality.pbworks.com>.

Jonietz, E. (2010, February 23). Augmented identity. MIT Technology Review.

Juhnke, J. Precise overlay registration within augmented reality—A glimpse into the technology. Tanagram.

Kato, H., & Billinghurst, M. (1999, October). Marker tracking and HMD calibration for a video-based augmented reality conferencing system. In Proceedings of the 2nd IEEE and ACM International Workshop on Augmented Reality (IWAR 99).

Kirkpatrick, M. (2009, August 24). Augmented reality: 5 barriers to a web that's everywhere. <Readwriteweb.com>.

Knowledge-based augmented reality (1993, July). <http://portal.acm.org/citation.cfm?id=159587>. ACM.

Kurzweil, R. (2005). The singularity is near Penguin Group.

Lomas, N. (2009, October). Cheat sheet: Augmented reality. <Silicon.com>.

Lomas, N. (2011, February). Augmented reality smartphones soar. <Silicon.com>.

Mackay, W. E. (1996). Augmenting reality: A new paradigm for interacting with computers. World Proceedings of ECSCW'93, the European Conference on Computer Supported Cooperative Work, vol. 7.

Matthew, W. G., Dye, C., Shawn, G., & Daphne, B. (2009, December). Increasing speed of processing with action video games. Current Directions in Psychological Science.

Media, B. (2010, February 2). The biggest challenge for augmented reality. Media Badger.

Michael, C., Markus, L., & Roger, R. (2010). The internet of things. McKinsey Quarterly.

Milgram, P., Takemura, H., Utsumi, A., & Kishino, F. (1994). Augmented reality: A class of displays on the reality-virtuality continuum. Telemanipulator and Telepresence Technologie (Vol. 2351, pp. 282–292).

Milgram, P., & Kishino, F. A taxonomy of mixed reality visual displays. In IEICE Transactions on Informations Systems 16, pp. 1–15.

Mims, C. (2010, July 2). Microsoft treating Cockroach Phobia with augmented reality. MIT Technology Review.

Mims, C. (2011, March 2). Are physical interfaces superior to virtual ones? MIT Technology Review.

Mims, C. (2011, April 7). Augmented reality interface exploits human nervous system. MIT Technology Review.

Mobile game aims to spice up the library (2008). Cable News Network.

Navab, N. (2001). Medical & industrial augmented reality: Challenges for real-time vision, Computer Graphics and Mobile Computing. *Computer Science,* 2191, 443–451.

Navab, N., et al.: Action- and workflow-driven augmented reality for computer-aided medical procedures. In IEE Computer Graphics and Applications, Jg. 2007, Heft September/October.

Navab, N., Bani-Hashemi, A., & Mitschke, M. (1999). Merging visible and invisible: Two camera-augmented mobile C-arm (CAMC) applications. In Proceedings, 2nd IEEE and ACM International Workshop on Augmented Reality (IWAR'99); Okt.; S. 134–141.

Parviz, B. (2009, September). Augmented reality contact lenses. IEEE Spectrum.

Perez, C. (2002). Technological revolutions and financial capital: The dynamics of bubbles and golden ages. Edward Elgar Publishing.

Pioneer Japan release the world first car in-dash GPS with augmented reality navigation (2011, May 9). <Akihabaranews.com>.

Popken, B. (2010, April). Augmented driving iPhone App gives your car a HUD. Consumerist.

Roman, F., Michael, P., & Alex, K. (2011). The rise of generation C. Strategy+Business. Spring.

Rosenberg, L. B. (1992). The use of virtual fixtures as perceptual overlays to enhance operator performance in remote environments. Technical Report AL-TR-0089, USAF Armstrong Laboratory, Wright-Patterson AFB OH.

Schrier, K. (2005, September). Revolutionizing history education: Using augmented reality games to teach histories. Massachusetts Institute of Technology.

Scott, J. (2009). Bringing books to life. MIT Technology Review. November/December.

Sen, P. (2010, June 25). Internet of things & augmented reality—challenges & opportunities. http://thinkplank.wordpress.com/2010/06/25/234/.

Sung, D. (2010, March 29). Will augmented reality change the way we see the future? Future Week.

Tofel, K. (2009, October 2). Challenges seen for augmented reality, but virtual future looks bright. <Gigaom.com>.

Vanillio, J. (1998, April). Introduction to augmented reality. Rochester Institute of Technology.

Vezina, K. (2011, August 17). Using games to get employees thinking. MIT Technology Review.

Video by Law, A., Ip, J., Visell, Y. (2010, April 29). Augmented-reality floor gives physical feedback. MIT Technology Review.

Wagner, D. History of mobile augmented reality. <www.icg.tugraz.at/~daniel/HistoryOfMobileAR>.

Williams, J. (2010, December). Augmented reality part two: Challenges & opportunities. <Hotstudio.com>.

<www.cnn.com/2011/TECH/innovation/04/01/new.york.library.game>.

Yapp, R. (2011, April 12). Brazilian police to use Robocop-style glasses at world cup the telegraph.

Index

Note: Page numbers followed by "f" and "t" indicate figures and tables respectively

Printed and bound by CPI Group (UK) Ltd, Croydon, CR0 4YY

03/10/2024

01040340-0004